CHANGE YOUR LIFE EACH DAY
(3 IN 1)

TRANSFORM YOUR INNER AND OUTER WORLD WITH
365 POSITIVE AFFIRMATIONS, DAILY ROUTINES FOR
HEALTHY HABITS & A YEAR OF GUIDED GRATITUDE
JOURNALING TO ATTRACT ABUNDANCE

NICOLE LOCKHART

SPECIAL BONUS!
Want this Bonus Book free?

Get **FREE**, unlimited access to it and all of my new books by joining the Fan Base!

  **SCAN WITH YOUR CAMERA TO JOIN!**

TABLE OF CONTENTS

HOW TO CHANGE YOUR HABITS
AND TRANSFORM YOUR LIFE

TABLE OF CONTENTS

---

365 DAYS OF POSITIVE AFFIRMATIONS

TABLE OF CONTENTS

One Year of Gratitude Journaling

HOW TO
CHANGE YOUR HABITS
AND TRANSFORM YOUR LIFE

A GUIDE TO BUILDING POSITIVE, DAILY ROUTINES TO
HELP MANIFEST THE LIFE YOU'VE ALWAYS WANTED

NICOLE LOCKHART

INTRODUCTION

Are you ready to make some changes to your Daily Habits to attract the life you've always wanted?

We all have a limited amount of energy to use up each day, will you choose to use it on healthy productive habits or will you let bad habits rob you of your best future and of reaching your dreams and goals?

After writing my last book, "365 Days of Positive Affirmations" all geared towards "change" in your life so that you can reach your big goals quickly and efficiently, I realized there was something else holding us back from using daily affirmations and reaching our goals quickly! Bad habits are keeping us stuck and the lack of new good habits are keeping us from speedily and consistently reaching our big goals!

The secrets of success are hiding behind our bad habits and routines. Bad habits trick us into thinking they're making us happy when they're really keeping us from achieving what we want most in life. Millions of people suffer from habits that are holding them back from their best lives. Obvious bad habits include drinking alcohol, smoking cigarettes, poor diet, not getting enough exercise or too much stress, but there are many others as well that are less obvious. Some are hard to identify and we don't even know how much they hold us back.

I am going to discuss the bad habits holding us back and some good habits to replace them. These are prominent areas that many people want to change in some way:

- Wealth
- Health and Healing
- Happiness
- Love and/or Meaningful Human Connection
- Self-Confidence and Self-Esteem
- Extreme Habits

If you have other areas in your life that you want to work on, no problem! These are just the top examples that I have found most people struggle with. You can use my methods and templates to change any habits and help you get to your goals faster!

I think most of us can agree that we all want more of these things in our life. But how to get there. It all starts with goals and plans. Dream big and make a list of your goals and dreams. Once you have your mind set on your destination, we will fill in the pieces to get you there. Imagine you are traveling across the country. You've never been there before but you have a destination. You have to take each mile at a time and focus on it to arrive safely. You need to check your directions along the way. The scenery will change and almost everything will change as you travel closer to your destination. You may have to alter your path if you go off course. And you will need to take time to rest along the way.

Bad habits are like getting a flat tire, not only once a day, but multiple times! Every time you get a flat tire you have to stop, probably spend some money, change the tire, and off you go again. Because habits are stored in the automatic part of your brain, you don't even question why you're doing them. Using the traveling analogy, you could question: maybe your tires aren't very good, maybe you're driving too fast or maybe you're on the wrong road altogether.

The same is true if your goal is a certain amount of money or a personal health target. Bad habits slow us down and use up our resources. PLEASE download my free book "Creating A Vision Board". This is will help you set some big goals, replace some of your bad habits with some productive ones, and begin to transform your life!

The Universe works like a magnet. Once you do the right work to yourself by changing your habits to be positive and productive, instead of negative and destructive, the things, people, relationships and everything else you've always wanted will come to you.

Daily habits can hold you back from the path to your dreams. So let's make sure you develop some good ones. You will learn to identify and get rid of old bad habits and replace them with good habits that benefit your life and your long-term goals.

CHAPTER 1:

WHY CHANGE YOUR HABITS?

What are habits, and how do they impact our life?

Change your habits and transform your life. It's no coincidence that the word "habit" is derived from the Latin word "habitare" which means "to dwell." Habits are something we do all day long, even when we're not aware of it. They offer a glimpse into our true selves: what we value, what scares us, and how much control we feel over our lives.

If you want to just add some positive, healthy habits into your life, then it is easy. Incorporate them into your daily routine and they will soon become automatic. If you are wanting to get rid of a bad habit, then it is a little more complicated and requires some perseverance, determination, willpower and a good plan!

We can cultivate positive habits to help us be happier and healthier or destructive ones to make us feel helpless. When changing a bad habit, there are three things to keep in mind:

- awareness (knowing which behaviors you want to change)
- motivation (having a reason why this new behavioral routine will benefit you in some way)

- and accountability (keeping track of your progress)

Daily habits are like tiny building blocks. Each day, are you building a healthy body? A good financial plan for your future? Every little thing you do is either building the thing you want or building something else. If you choose a donut for a snack instead of a piece of fruit, you are building an unhealthy body, not a healthy one. If you spend your money frivolously on fancy dining and entertaining nights out you are building a less than robust financial future for yourself, instead of a solid and profitable one.

How do Habits form?

Habits become your routine. The more you do them, the harder they are to break. You may already have some good habits, like keeping your kitchen clean or eating a good diet. But you may want to identify some habits that are hindering your ultimate plan to reaching your goals and living your best life.

Habits can start off as part of a conscious goal but quickly become automatic and subconscious. The American Journal of Psychology defines a "habit" as a more or less fixed way of thinking, willing, or feeling acquired through previous repetition of a mental experience. New behaviors can become automatic through the process of habit formation. The behavioral patterns of habit become imprinted in neural pathways, making old habits hard to break and new ones hard to form, but by using repetition, new habits can form and replace bad ones.

Habit formation has three main parts, the context cue, the behavioral repetition and the reward. This is known as the habit loop. We will talk about breaking or changing the habit loop in the coming Chapters.

Recognizing and eliminating bad habits as soon as possible is advised because as we age the habits become more ingrained in our neural pathways. It doesn't mean that you will be stuck with a bad habit forever, it just requires more effort to change or replace a long-standing bad habit.

We all have a certain amount of energy to expend each day. Will you choose to use it on habits that leave you feeling unhealthy, broke, alone and hopeless? Or will you make an effort to only expend your daily energy on habits that promote a healthy body, solid financial future and a life full of meaningful relationships?

Qualities of Good Habits

*They benefit you. Are your daily habits contributing to a healthy body and mind? Are you making choices that your future self will be proud of? Are you saving money for your future? Do you have a balance of rest and work?

*They benefit others. Anytime win-win is at work, you know you have a good habit. Good habits are often synergistic, they are good for you and good for others.

*They are enjoyable. When you start a new habit it might not feel that enjoyable right away, there might be a period of mourning for your old destructive habit. But in time your positive habit will be enjoyable. For example, walking or running every day. At first, you might be missing your couch, but in time you will get used to the endorphins and good feelings that come from walking or running regularly.

*They are productive. They produce a healthy body, mind or benefit your life in some way. They are often forward-looking and contribute to your big picture and long-term goals.

*They involve action. They involve "doing" something. I don't mean watching TV or social media, I mean creating something, caring for yourself or someone else, and thinking of your future.

*They promote your health. Good health habits might seem obvious, but you might need some help identifying which of your health habits are actually good habits. You will be able to use the templates in Chapter 10 to help you become aware of some of your health habits.

*They have a long-term goal attached to themselves. Many good habits will pay off in the future. Exercising daily, eating healthily, saving money, all will benefit your future self.

*They are honest and have integrity. Good habits are always honest and true. Not just true for you but true for the Universe. Good habits are universally good and are based on strong moral principles.

*They encourage self-discipline. By choosing to focus on creating good habits, it will help you when temptation arises. Self-discipline is a muscle, the more you use it, the stronger it gets.

*They are constructive with your big picture goals. Good habits will help you build the future that you've always wanted. You may not see results right away, but rest assured, your good habits are building blocks for your best future self and life.

Qualities of Bad habits

*They harm you or others. Some habits such as smoking or over-eating are pretty obviously bad for your own body. But there are many other habits that aren't as clear, cut and dried. You might think your habit isn't harming anyone other than yourself, but when you dig a little deeper, you will see that most habits that harm yourself, will also have an effect down the line of harming others. Second-hand smoke is an obvious one and for over-eating, your friends and family might be missing out on a healthy energetic "you".

*They destroy synergy. Bad habits are not synergistic. They are the opposite, they repulse others that would otherwise be good friends or companions away from us, and we end up with others that share our bad habits.

*They are not productive. Over time our bad habits leave us with nothing. Our bodies become unhealthy, our bank accounts become empty and you have nothing to show from all your daily habit energy.

*They cost you your health or your money. Most bad habits will end up costing you your health or your money at some point. It may not seem obvious when you're young and full of youthful energy, but over time, bad habits take a toll.

*They are destructive of your big picture goals. Bad habits will keep you pacified for today but will they create the future you've always dreamt of having? No, they will not. They rob you of your dreams and goals, not right away but long-term you will be left with nothing and only then you will see what bad habits have stolen from you. Let me help you be proactive today so that you can have the future that you've always wanted.

CHAPTER 2:

WHY IS IT SO HARD TO CHANGE YOUR HABITS?

"Old habits die hard." The only way to win against this old quote is perseverance and a good plan. You need to pull out all the stops and use affirmations, visualizations, lists and the templates in Chapter 10 of this book. You need to develop your perseverance and willpower. You will become stronger and stronger as you take it one day at a time.

Awareness is a good place to begin, start thinking about when your bad habits creep in, when does it happen, who are you with, where are you, what is the trigger/cue, does it happen right after something else? Practice mindfulness, simply observe the impulses that relate to your bad habit without judging or reacting, just become aware and write them down.

Changing anything can be hard. Our brains become wired to think something is normal and then when you suddenly change it, your brain is left with a gap. It feels like something is missing. Sometimes we know a habit is bad for us, but our brains will fight as if our existence depended on perpetuating the bad habit. The habit-forming behaviors are linked to the basal-ganglia, also known as the "autopilot" part of our brain. No wonder it is so hard to break them!

Breaking the Habit loop.

The best way to change anything is to REPLACE it with something more powerful and positive. In the next chapter, you will learn the 3 parts of habits. The context cue, the behavioral routine and the reward and will talk about replacing one or all of the parts to break the bad habit cycle. This is why "just say no" doesn't work. The right answer is "just say yes" to a more positive routine that fulfills the reward of your cue or trigger.

New routines could include:
Choosing gum to replace a cigarette, when you get the smoking urge
Choosing a piece of fruit to replace a sugary snack, when you have a sugar craving
Going for a walk to replace lying on the couch, when you get home from work

Another reason why it is so hard is because most of us don't do it right. A big thing many of us get wrong is positive vs. negative phrasing.

Many studies have shown that positive phrasing is more powerful than negative phrasing. Remember this when you choose the habits that you want to start changing. Be patient with yourself and always think of the positive thing you are gaining instead of the negative thing you are trying to get rid of or stop doing.

How to phrase your goals in a positive way:
A classic example is the notoriously bad habit of smoking. Instead of making your goal "to quit smoking" make it "to have pink, clean, healthy lungs".

Instead of making your goal "to be less lazy" make your goal "to find exercise that I enjoy".

Instead of making your goal "to stop being broke all the time" make your goal "to earn a certain amount of money that will cover all my needs".

By phrasing your goals and routines positively, you are incredibly helping your subconscious to help you reach your goals. Your brain doesn't know what to do with negatives, it gets stuck and just goes in circles. All your brain hears is "smoke, lazy, broke". Your mind gets confused as to why you would want to focus on those things. But with positive goals, your mind hears "clean, healthy, exercise, money" and it's full speed ahead to achieve success!

Now that you are committed to making some habit changes to help you reach your big picture goals, help your brain even more by making some colorful posters that envision your new habit. Write down some of your favorite positive affirmations to get you there faster and more efficiently.

What causes Bad Habits?

Stress, boredom and loneliness are the main causes of bad habits. The "habit loop" starts often when we are young and becomes stronger and stronger as the years go by. The basal ganglia part of our brain is not only linked to habits but also to the development of emotions, memories and pattern recognition. This is helpful for productive automatic routines like brushing your teeth or parallel parking, but not for destructive habits.

Once a specific behavior becomes automatic, our free will and decision-making part of our brain, the prefrontal cortex, thinks that these automatic behaviors are taking care of themselves and turns off from recognizing them so it can focus on other day-to-day decisions. Your prefrontal cortex doesn't distinguish between good automatic behaviors and bad automatic behaviors.

Often bad habits can start because we are trying to fill a void. Maybe you didn't get support or love from your parents and started smoking or eating too much junk food. Many bad habits stem back decades and you will have to go back in time to discover the motivations for starting. Once you've done that, you can try to find some replacement habits that fulfill the need that was never fulfilled to start with. Use Template 3 in Chapter 10.

Conditions that require professional help.

This book is not a replacement for medical or professional help. These are some conditions that you will likely need additional support to overcome.

Compulsions and Obsessive-Compulsive Disorder (OCD). Compulsive acts can start when someone tries to fight their anxious or intrusive thoughts with a purposeful, deliberate action (can be physical or mental). The behavior soon becomes automatic and can be overwhelming and consuming.

Addictions and substance use. These conditions can start off recreationally and quickly lead to a more serious dependency-like condition. You will likely need professional help to stop these cases.

Smoking. Some people can stop smoking on their own, but many require multiple layers of support including counseling or medication from a medical doctor. Smoking can start as a bad habit but soon becomes a physical and psychological dependency situation.

Eating disorders. Any type of eating disorder should not be taken lightly. They can stem from bad eating habits and soon evolve into sometimes life-threatening conditions. Seek professional help if you have any type of eating disorder.

We will talk more about these conditions in Chapter 9.

The False feeling of Deserving.

Have you ever felt like you deserved that extra drink because you worked hard, or felt like you deserved a piece of cake because you exercised last week? I have been studying deserving for a while and it is easy to see the downside of it just by looking at some specific celebrities. I won't mention any names but numerous big stars have ended up addicted, cheating on their spouses, wasting their money, or just wasting their lives in general. When they finally reach rock bottom and are able to talk about what has happened, time and time again, they say "I felt like I deserved it". Meaning they deserved the mistresses, drugs and phony good times because of who they are and their acclaimed celebrity success. Feeling like you deserve can also lead to developing bad habits and in extreme cases, addiction, substance use and other life-wasting conditions. Try to change your mindset about deserving.

Grace.

Instead of "deserving" think "grace". Grace might sound religious to you, but it didn't start out that way, it is a very old word with Latin origin. The Merriam-Webster dictionary says grace is "unmerited divine assistance given to humans for their regeneration or sanctification", or "a state of sanctification enjoyed through divine assistance".

Grace is letting the Universe fit you in where you belong. By trusting that the Universe will put you in the way of many good things will in fact, ensure that the benefits/rewards of your hard work are positive, healthy and satisfy your life goals. When we make up our own benefits/rewards because we think we deserve them, time and time again we choose wrong.

I am not saying don't strive for your new car, house, or life partner. That is exactly what I want you to have. Set big goals and find your way to get them. But HOW you get them is important. If you feel "deserving" you might be tempted to cut corners or choose the quick-fix way to your goal, or completely forget your goal because of some short-term good times. Keep your eye on the prize. Set your big goals and change your habits to get there safely and as soon as possible without wasting time. Have faith that the Universe is helping you.

It is no coincidence that "grace" and "gratitude" start with the same three letters. Both of these words come from Latin origin meaning "pleasing, thankful". Developing a grateful attitude will ensure you are living a graceful life, attuned to the Universe, where all your dreams and goals can become reality. You can use my book "One Year of Gratitude Journaling" to get started.

Make your own luck.

People that are attuned to the universe and living in a graceful state are sometimes seen as being "lucky". Good things just seem to happen regularly for people living like this. The good news is, you can make your own luck! When you dig deep and find out what really makes you happy and which long-term goals you want to achieve, get yourself on the right path, and practice gratitude, everything will fall into place. Things will just start working out for you, and you will have good fortune not just from chance, but because you put yourself in the path of all the good things that you want in life.

When you are doing all the right steps to manifesting your goals, you are walking in grace, the Universe will give you what you need, when you need it. Trust that by doing the right work upfront, and being patient, the Universe will pull your goals to you like a magnet, all in perfect and due time. And when you get them the right way, they will stick to you magnetically.

CHAPTER 3:

THE BEST WAYS TO
CHANGE YOUR HABITS.

What is preventing you from getting to your Big Goals? Do you need more money? A healthier body? More time to meet people? Try to find the negative thing that you do regularly that is hindering your progress to your goals. Read through the "bad habits" listed for each of the following Chapters. There will be some things that you are doing daily you might not even realize are keeping you from reaching your goals.

Chapter 10 of this book, has some templates to help you identify the habits that you want to change and help you keep on track when developing new ones. Make written or visual plans for changing your habits, make as many as you need and put them in places where you will see them regularly.

Break the Cycle

Every habit is based on a cycle: the context cue, the behavioral repetition (routine) and the reward/benefit. Or the 3 R's reminder (cue), routine, reward. This is known as the habit loop.

First, become aware of your bad habit:

1. Identify the cue for your bad habit (ex. break time at work, needing a sugar rush for energy when you are hungry and craving a donut)
2. Identify the routine (eating the donut at break time)
3. Identify the reward (energy and a full stomach)

Once you have identified these three characteristics of your bad habit, you can try to eliminate the cue if possible. In this case, the cue can't be eliminated so the next option is changing a bad habit routine. Replace the middle step (the routine) with something positive that satisfies the reward. Make a list of possible choices. Once you feel the cue/trigger coming on, check out your list and have an arsenal of healthy choices waiting in the wings. A banana is high in healthy sugar, potatoes and starchy fruits and vegetables can also satisfy a sugar craving in a healthy way.

Here are some different approaches to eliminating bad habits and forming new ones. They can be used together or separately, some may work for some habits and some may not. As you learn more about yourself, your habits and your motivations for eliminating habits and forming new ones, you will get clearer on how to use these strategies. Be sure to use the Templates in Chapter 10 to help you make a plan to break some old habits and form some new ones.

Remove the Cue/Urge/Trigger.

This is also known as *withdrawal of reinforcers* – identifying and removing factors that trigger and reinforce the habit. If you have a drinking problem, don't go to the bar, if you have a sweet tooth don't bring sugary snacks into the house and leave them lying around. This will make it easier for you as you form new habits to replace old ones.

Change or alter your environment and avoid, avoid, avoid. Write out some one-liners if your habit has a social basis so that you are ready when you're asked to put yourself in an environment that contributes to or triggers your bad habit.

If you can't eliminate the Cue, replace the Routine and add in more Rewards.

Some cues we can't eliminate, for example getting home after work, can trigger us to feel like lying on the couch. Although we can't eliminate this cue, we can replace the routine by going for a walk instead of lying on the couch.

Here is an example of how to make a positive habit-changing statement to hang on your wall where you feel your cue, in this case, the entrance hall.

1. Identify the cue, when and where does it happen?
2. Identify the routine you want to change and phrase it in a positive way about what you are gaining, instead of what you are giving up. Write it down.

   Example: "I want to get more exercise" (Instead of "I feel tired and want to lie on the couch")

3. Add in some benefits/rewards to your statement.

   Example: "I want to get more exercise so that I have more energy and to be healthy."

   Example: "When I get home from work, I feel like lying on the couch."

Replace it with: "When I get home from work I feel like going for a 10-minute power walk so I will have energy and feel healthy."

4. Now that you know what to do, put your plan (using Template 5) up on the wall near your front door. For this habit, the cue happens around 4:30 pm each day, so be ready. When your cue comes up at 4:30 it's time for the Big Guns, keep your templates, vision board and positive affirmations by your front door, before you even take your shoes off, go for your walk!

In addition to the specific habits listed for each topic in the following Chapters, the best things you can do daily once you have created some big goals, is to create a vision board for your goals and use daily positive affirmations to re-program your brain.

Visualization. Studies have shown that there is a super-power to visualization. You've probably heard about the basketball experiment by Australian psychologist Alan Richardson. He divided players into three groups and did an experiment for 20 days. The first group practiced free throws every day. The second group did free throws on the first and 20th day as did the third group. But the third group visualized their free throws for 20 minutes a day for days 2-19. When it came time to test the progress on the 20th day, the first group had improved by 24%, the second group not at all, and the third group improved 23%! Nearly the same as the actual practicing group. Visualization is powerful for your success, take some time to surround yourself with photos that describe your new habits and lifestyle. Then spend a certain amount of time each day envisioning yourself doing your new habit.

You can also visualize yourself breaking a bad habit and envision yourself reacting differently. This is a good time to practice some deep breathing exercises as you might feel anticipation or nervousness. You can use a fidget toy if you need help staying calm and repeat some of your favorite affirmations as well.

Positive Affirmations are like snow tires in the blizzard of life. Now that you have identified some habits that you want to change, phrased them positively, added in some benefits and are aware of your bad habit cue and routine, I suggest using positive affirmations to make your new habit easier to achieve. Once you are on the path to your goals, affirmations will get you there faster and safely with no chance of going off the track. By repeating some well-thought-out and well-chosen affirmations, your brain will become effectively reprogrammed. It will think the things you are wanting are now normal and the Universe will bring them to you.

What the mind can conceive and believe it can achieve. Your brain is the original super-computer, if you are not where you currently want to be in your life, it's time for some reprogramming. I have listed some of my favorite and most powerful positive affirmations after each chapter. Choose your favorites and write them on a piece of paper but them in your bathroom, kitchen, or car so that you can see them regularly throughout the day. You can also read my book "365 Days of Positive Affirmations" for a daily guide and added ammunition for this journey you are embarking on to create the life that you want. Affirmations are always spoken in the present tense. This way your brain hears the affirmation as if it is already happening. You believe it is happening before it is your reality and the thing you are wanting is magnetically drawn to you.

Doing a 180.

Limiting beliefs keep us stuck. The best way to combat limiting beliefs is with positive affirmations. If you are wanting to get more exercise because you feel overweight or have no energy, tell yourself "I am fit and am full of energy." This is sort of like using positive affirmations but it is an "opposite" affirmation activity. If you think you are not a good cook, tell yourself "I am a good cook." This will make your brain think you really are a good cook and you will start feeling more adventurous and productive in the kitchen.

This might seem a bit odd that you're telling yourself, "I am rich", when you're struggling to pay your bills. Your conscious mind knows that it doesn't reflect your current reality. But your subconscious mind is hard at work and doesn't realize that it is not your current reality. All your powerful subconscious hears is "I am rich", you will start to feel like it is a part of who you are and riches and wealth will soon be drawn to you.

Make a list of the habits that you want to change and tackle them one at a time.

You might not know where to start. You might be wanting a certain lifestyle but not know how to get there. That's ok! Take some time to get to know yourself, your bad habits and your good ones. Use Template 2 in Chapter 10 to identify some bad habits that you may want to change. Tackle them one by one.

Be patient with yourself, allow slip-ups.

We are all human, two steps forward, one step back is reality sometimes. Slip-ups happen. Use a growth mindset, tell yourself *"next time* I will do it differently", "I haven't been able to do it *yet*", *"but* I'm working hard to reach my goals."

It took a long time to build your habits and it will take some time and dedication to break them.

Self-discipline and good old-fashioned willpower will grow with time and practice, just like a muscle. Template 7 will help you become aware of why you had a slip-up and help you come up with a plan for *next time*.

Join forces with someone that has the same habit or lifestyle goals.

Find a friend, someone that wants to go to the gym with you every day or hang out and watch movies on the weekend to avoid public houses, etc. If your habits are deeper and more dangerous you will need to seek help from a professional. Serious conditions include compulsions, substance use, addiction, or emotional eating.

Reminders.

Set yourself up for success, if you are hooked on social media, invest in some crafts, books, journals and other activities to keep you busy. Place them ahead of time in the places where you scroll for hours on your phone or computer. Put sticky notes with affirmations and reminders in spots where you are triggered to start an unhealthy habit. Or put pieces of fruit waiting for you where you might sit when you crave a sugary snack.

Baby steps. It's not all or nothing.

Eliminating habits and forming new ones is a progression so celebrate the baby steps. If your goal is to stop smoking, keep track of lowering the daily amount of cigarettes that you smoke each day. If you can get down to one, then you can come up with some new ideas to stop completely. If you are working on forming a new habit of eating fruit daily, celebrate each day you remember to do your new habit. Use the Templates in Chapter 10, Template 8 for Bad Habit Daily Progress and Template 10 for Good Habit Daily Progress.

Take a vacation.

If you want to break a bad habit, do it on a holiday. When you are on a holiday, your environment is changed so much that your cues, routines and rewards are all different as well. Everything is out of order, it is a naturally good time to break a habit loop and replace some routines or avoid a cue altogether.

How long does it take to break a habit?

It used to be thought that most habits could be changed in about 21 days but now most experts agree it takes about 10 weeks (about 2-3 months) of repetition and dedication to break a habit. Each habit will be different and depend on how long you've had the habit, the emotional or physical needs of your habit, whether or not you have support and the physical or emotional reward the habit provides.

For Chapters 4-8, I have listed bad habits first and then some good ones that you can use to replace bad habits if you are not already doing them. I've listed the bad habits first because bad habits are the problem!

No one ever complains about good habits ruining their life. If you can replace a bad habit with a good one, it's a double gain, losing the bad one and gaining the good one. I know you can do it! Use the templates in Chapter 10, positive affirmations, visualization and all the other ideas contained in this book and don't give up until your new habit wins out!

Positive Affirmations for Change

"Change happens quickly and easily."

"I let go of all that doesn't serve me, to make room for new healthy routines."

"I have everything I need to change my life."

"I am ready for change."

"I am filled with trust that change will happen and bring good into my life."

"I am in control of my life."

"I make changes in my life to bring me joy and happiness."

"I have the power to create my reality."

"I now step out of my comfort zone to become the person I've always wanted to be."

"I attract people that support me."

"I choose to live my best life."

"I attract people that help me grow."

"I adapt well to the changes I am making."

CHAPTER 4:

HABITS FOR WEALTH

Many people dream of wealth. Many of us also wonder why we haven't achieved this goal. We work hard every day, so where is the wealth and luxurious lifestyle we dream of? The only tried, tested and true way to earn money is to provide a valuable service or product to others. It's that simple. Money isn't just for lucky people, it's for people that have a plan and work hard on their plan every day! It may not look like rich people work hard but this is because they have the privilege of having people and systems in place working for them. They can leverage their own time by having others do the work for them. But for most of us, we've got a ways to go before we can employ others to do our work for us.

In order to create the financial life that you've always dreamt of, you need only 2 things, a goal and a plan. And good old-fashioned hard work of course. Riches most effectively come to you if you can name an exact amount and then make your plan to get it.

If your goal is $10,000, or more, or less. You can have it! You just need a plan. Here are some ideas:

GOAL: $10,000

PLAN OPTIONS:

*Build and sell, 100 wooden coffee tables and sell them for 100$ each.

*Start a YouTube channel and learn about monetizing your video(s).

*Start a business doing what you are passionate about. Example: selling original artwork. You could sell 200 prints at 50$ each (minus expenses).

*Provide a valuable service. Perhaps a delivery service or yard care.

Make a vision board and use color and sparkles to super-charge your brain. Put "$10,000" on your board, put pictures of the things you will buy and do with the money, and also put pictures of the work that you will do to earn this money.

There are endless options and the right one for you should be based on what you enjoy. Then when tough times arise, as they always will. You will be more positive, resilient and quickly be able to pick yourself up and carry on. Think about the traveling analogy, if/when your car breaks down: if you are really excited about where you are going, you will get it fixed quickly and get back on your journey, if you are not excited about your destination, you might sit around for a while and use the car problem as an excuse to stall on your path to your goals.

Once you start earning extra income to reach your lifestyle goals, it is just important to keep that money. Let's have look at some bad wealth habits and some good ones that we can replace them with.

Old Bad Habits

Wasting time. You don't have to look far to find time wasters, social media and TV probably top the list. There is so much available to us via streaming or regular broadcasting, you might not realize this is a huge time waster. Do something that involves sharpening your brain, increasing the health of your body, or spend time executing or strategizing your plans for wealth.

Not keeping track of spending. It is very easy to lose track of where all that hard-earned money goes. A few fancy coffee drinks per week adds up to a lot of money. Money that could be spent paying down your credit cards or put towards your future.

Shopping sales or impulse buys. Some people just can't help buying something that is on sale. I personally know a few. They will come home stocked up with things they never needed in the first place because it was on sale.

Not saving. Try to save 10-20% of your income for your future. Get a separate bank account and sock it away there. If this doesn't work, you can put actual bills somewhere you won't be able to easily access them. You can also buy silver or gold coins or bars. These will go up in value and are not as easily spent as regular currency.

Relying on one stream of income. We have all seen in recent years how quickly things can change and you can be left with no job overnight. Try to start up a side-gig of sorts. Providing a valuable product or a service to others will guarantee some extra income.

Procrastinating. This is one of the most common and most crippling bad habits! The time is now, make a to-do list and work at checking those things off.

Not focussing. Set some big money goals, you can use my free "Creating A Vision Board" book and I would recommend my book "365 Days of Positive Affirmations" to help you find out what you really want in life. You need to feed your desire for riches and make it so strong that wealth has no choice but to come to you.

Giving up. Many people give up on their plans and goals when they haven't even given them a fair chance. The thing is, you can never tell how far you are from reaching your goal. It could be a ways off or it could be just around the corner. So don't quit! Your goals and dreams are closer than you might think.

New Good Habits

Provide a valuable product or service. As discussed earlier, this is the only sustainable way to riches. Keep brainstorming practical ideas for you. Find side-gigs that use your gifts and talents to provide a valuable product or service to others.

Being an early riser. It's hard to be productive when you don't start your day early. This is why nearly half of the self-made millionaires get up at least 3 hours before their 9-5 starts. This helps them tackle personal projects or plan for what will come next with a clear head, free from distractions like email notifications popping up onscreen while working. Also, when you wake up at the crack of dawn, it gives you a sense of power over your life. You're in control and can tackle anything that comes along with this newfound good habit.

Practicing gratitude daily. Being grateful for the things you have brings more of the things you want into your life. You can use my book "One Year of Gratitude Journaling" or just write down what you are grateful for on a piece of paper daily.

The best sleep is before midnight. This goes hand in hand with getting up early. My grandfather from the Old country in Europe used to say the best sleep is before midnight. He was right, your circadian rhythm wants you to sleep when it's dark and get up at the crack of dawn. Try to incorporate this good habit to increase your productivity.

Building multiple streams of income. Most of us have a 9-5 job. Whether we love it, hate it, or somewhere in the middle, relying solely on one income stream is a dicey way to go. As evidenced in the last few years, things can change quickly. Prepare today so that if your primary source of income disappears you will have a backup plan. You can provide a valuable product or service to others, start up a YouTube channel or start a business doing a hobby that you love. Brainstorm to find something that you enjoy that can also earn you money.

Setting priorities. Most of us do not have any priorities. Setting goals is a great way to motivate yourself, but it's hard if you don't know where your money should go or how much is enough for any given goal. Using your finances, you can invest in your future. What are your priorities? Retiring early? Saving to put your kids through college? Traveling the world? Add some photos that represent these things to your vision board. We all have different priorities, and we need financial planning tools to help sometimes. There are also personal planners for hire and Apps to give you some advice.

Saving and then spending. You should start your month by securing savings and investments - at least 20% of what you make. Spend from what is left. Warren Buffett once said, "Save First, Spend Later". It makes perfect sense if you don't want to be left with nothing at the end of your month.

Investing. Maintaining a monthly investment contribution is necessary to grow wealth, especially if other debts or expenses are coming up. So, the first step towards building healthy finances is to make sure you're continuously investing wisely each month. Set money aside in a retirement fund, buy safe securities on the stock market or get advice from a trusted financial planner.

Managing your time. A day has only 24 hours. If you're looking for success, then it's essential to understand how much time each task will take. Whether you want more money in your pocket or just some extra cash, you must utilize your resources efficiently and effectively and not waste any time. To have a productive day, keep your focus on the tasks at hand by making lists, and checking them off as completed or undone and prioritize based on importance. Using online tools may also help. If you need to, buy an analog clock or an old-school wristwatch so that you can see the seconds ticking by. Get to work now!

Building your team. On your road to wealth and success, you will need many people to help you along the way. And they are worth their weight in gold. The person that does some of your behind-the-scenes work for you, the person that encourages you to keep going, or the person at the shop that gives a good deal on supplies. Treat your team well, they are invaluable. People are more likely to help you if they feel like a valued member of your team. A respectful attitude towards others attracts opportunities that can turn into cash, so stay humble and be grateful.

Avoiding late fees. Automate your bill payments. Don't let late payments ruin your finances. Avoid these expensive mistakes by automating every bill with apps available today so you never have to worry about them again. It will help you get closer to achieving your goals quickly, while saving money along the way.

Making a list for expenditures. Creating a list and sticking by it can help you avoid impulse buys or picking up items that may not be necessary. Having an idea of what you need on your shopping trips will help you stay focused and not distracted by sales. Buying online can be a fantastic way to save money as well. You'll quickly get a sense of what you need and how much it will cost to buy. When making purchases online, wait at least 24 hours before committing. You may change your mind. As important as it is to earn the amount of money that you have been dreaming about, it is just as important to keep it.

Starting retirement plans as early as possible. An individual must plan if they want their life after their working years (or decades) to be filled with happiness and joy. Invest wisely because there have been some real bumps along the way, financially speaking, in the last few years. One way to prepare for retirement is by investing in physical assets, like real estate. Not only will this give you passive income from rent, but it could also be an attractive long-term investment opportunity with low risk.

A bonus tip: Take care of your health. As the old adage goes, "if wealth is lost, something is lost, but if health is lost, everything is lost". In the next chapter, you will learn about creating some good habits for maintaining health and promoting healing.

Positive Affirmations for Wealth

"Wealth is drawn to me like a magnet."

"Having enough money for everything I want is normal for me."

"Money comes to me quickly and easily."

"I give valuable services or products in exchange for money."

"Prosperity and success come naturally to me."

"I attract the riches that I desire."

"The money I spend goes to valuable places and comes back to me multiplied."

"I am always increasing my income."

"I am always thinking of new ways to earn money."

"I am good at managing my finances and easily reach my financial goals."

"I am a money magnet."

"Money comes to me in unexpected ways."

"I have an unlimited source of income in my life."

CHAPTER 5:

HABITS FOR HEALTH AND HEALING

Lifestyle changes fall into three categories:

- Behavioral: planning activities, sleeping habits, and physical activity
- Dietary: water intake and a nutritious diet
- Psychological: attitude, mood, and stress management

By simply incorporating some new habits into your daily routine, you can create personal health like never before. If you want to replace a bad habit routine with a healthy new one, use Template 5 to help you get started. Let's discuss a few essential habit changes here.

Old Bad Habits

Giving in to laziness. We all feel tired at the end of a long workday. Resting at the right time is important, but don't be deceived, physical exercise is the trick to getting more energy. It is also the best way to heal your body and maintain your body as you age. When we exercise so many great things happen, your body is filled with oxygen, (which has been linked to preventing diseases including cancer), it boosts your metabolism to help control an ideal weight, it promotes your sleep, increases your mood, it can be fun and many other benefits.

The more you do it, the easier and more enjoyable it will get. So don't get sucked into your couch after a long day of work, go for a short walk!

Eating sugar. Refined sugar is maybe the worst invention in modern history. It can lead to diabetes, cancer and a multitude of other morbid illnesses. It also stimulates the same part of the brain as many drugs and has been shown to be more addictive than cocaine! Sugar affects our cognitive skills and also our self-control. The addiction-like effects caused by sugar can cause, over-eating, loss of self-control and even memory loss. Processed food contains a ton of refined sugar! Try to become more aware of what you are eating by reading the ingredients lists on the food you buy. If you have a sweet tooth already, try eating all kinds of fruit! The sugar in fruit is completely different from white or refined sugar, so try to find some different kinds of fruit that you enjoy!

Living under stress. Many of us have been under stress for so long that we don't know life to be any different. Some symptoms of too much stress in your life are insomnia, low energy, depression, acne, headaches, chronic pain, frequent illness, digestive issues and weight gain to name a few. Sound familiar? Some new habits include: getting enough sleep, exercising, eliminating stressors, lowering your caffeine and sugar intake, finding like-minded positive people to be around, meditation and deep breathing exercises.

Not giving your body what it needs. Your body wants to be healthy and heal. It is yearning for exercise and good food. Try to spend some time alone to listen to what your individual body needs and give it to yourself!

Taking drugs or alcohol. Putting any of these things in our bodies is not healthy, but in moderation, can reduce stress and cause enjoyment for some people. Substance use can be mild and recreational or become a more serious dependency. When the use becomes overpowering in a way that harms you or leads you to harm others like your family or friends in some way, then it is problematic. You will need to seek professional help to overcome this condition.

Over-eating. There is a Confucian teaching called Hara hachi bun me, which means eat until you are 80% full. It originated in Okinawa, Japan as a way to control eating habits. Okinawans interestingly have one of the lowest rates of illness from cancer, heart disease and stroke. Also, slow down when you're eating to give your body a chance to register how much you have eaten. Eating until you are "80% satisfied" instead of "full" has numerous health benefits. If you struggle with under-eating try to eat small portions more often, and seek professional help if you need to.

Smoking. Unfortunately, many people get hooked on this one when they are young and as the years go by it gets harder and harder to stop. You might need professional help to stop smoking and replace it with a healthy habit that includes some irresistible healthy rewards. Medical doctors can prescribe medication that can help, deep breathing and exercise have also been shown to be effective in combatting this bad habit.

New Good Habits

Getting quality Sleep. The correct amount of sleep can make a world of difference. A lack of good sound sleep affects the way your brain works, which in turn causes more problems. Getting enough sleep can help you protect not only mental but also physical health. Sleep helps the body regenerate, increases healthy brain function and maintains overall wellbeing. You must try to go to sleep at the same time every day. Keep your sleep schedule consistent on weeknights and weekends. Keep the bedroom dark, and don't watch TV or use screens before bedtime as they may signal your brain that it's time for action. Again, the old saying "The best sleep is before midnight" holds true today. Our body's circadian rhythm is dependant on light, so go to bed early and get up when the sun rises.

Moving and getting exercise. Optimum health cannot be achieved without physically moving around. A sedentary life has been linked to health problems like weight gain and heart disease. Be active, preferably for at least 30 minutes a day, every day to achieve your fitness goals. Evening walking or light jogging is a good starting habit to create. Not only that but those who are more physically engaged live longer too. If you currently do not exercise, start by doing some just once or twice per week at first, and gradually build longer routines up over time. There are so many kinds of enjoyable exercise to choose from, walking, running, swimming, weight lifting, rock climbing, dancing, yoga, aerobics, to name a few.

Cleaning your living space. If you are trying to kick a pesky bad habit and are not sure what to replace it with, cleaning your living environment is a fantastic habit to form and has numerous benefits. You can get great exercise from cleaning, it has a calming effect on your mind and it makes you feel happy to live in a clean environment.

Getting outside. Any kind of exercises are great habits to form, but there is something about being outside in nature, that has an extra deep calming effect. Sitting in nature can also help you to listen to your inner voice and figure out what makes you happy and what your long-term goals are. Fresh air and oxygen are essential for health and healing.

Drinking more water. The benefits to drinking more water are endless, this is a habit that you'll want to do multiple times in a day. Drinking more water has been shown to stabilize your heartbeat, regulate blood pressure, cushion your joints, aid in digestion, add energy and a ton of others benefits. Most adults need about 4-6 cups a day, around a liter. It is possible to drink too much water if you have certain health conditions including thyroid, kidney, liver, or heart problems or if you take some medications such as non-steroidal anti-inflammatory drugs (NSAIDs). Consult a doctor about water intake if you have a serious condition. But for most people, more water is the way to go!

Practicing good dietary habits. Eat more fruits and veggies for a healthy digestive system. Fruits and vegetables are rich in antioxidants, and contain fiber that helps you feel full longer, keeping your appetite under control. That's why the American Heart Association recommends filling at least half your plate with fruits or veggies every day so you can reach 4 ½ cups per day total! You can choose: canned, fresh, or frozen vegetables as they all count toward meeting this goal. Researchers have found a diet high in fruit and vegetables is capable of protecting against cancer, diabetes, and heart disease. Don't eat junk food and try to cut back on processed foods. Making smoothies is a great daily habit that easily incorporates more fruits and veggies into your diet.

Relaxing. Take out time for yourself. You can't give your all to everything if you're not taking care of yourself. Self-care should be refreshing and calming. Focusing on self-care will help make sure you don't burn out. Try to maintain good habits such as exercising regularly. Meditation, yoga, reading and many others can also be relaxing positive habits.

Putting limits on social media. Do not let social media take the better part of your life. Limit your time exposure on social media. Try to make rules like "no phones in the bedroom" after dinner time" etc., to help implement keeping away from social media. Or you can change "My Phone Settings" by going into Settings > Screen Time and restricting usage for apps during certain hours so that there is downtime each day. Small things go a long way. Try it out.

Being Disciplined. There is nothing more important than discipline when trying to create optimum personal health. Eating the right food and exercising can be vital to living a healthy lifestyle. But if you're not disciplined, it's all for nothing, no matter what type of diet or exercise routine you choose. To improve your health, change your mindset. A lack of discipline makes achieving long-term goals nearly impossible. Any successful habit requires a consistent investment of your time and effort. Use your vision board, positive affirmations and the templates in Chapter 10, to help keep you on track when forming your new habits.

Doing Crossword Puzzles. Long before Alzheimer's or Dementia became an issue, researchers found that mentally challenging activities may offer protection against the risk of these diseases. Playing games like chess and solving puzzles regularly, as well as, engaging your mind with reading can help lower chances in those prone to develop these conditions. Though there is no cure yet, prevention through different methods such as eating certain foods ensures less likelihood of cognitive decline later down the line. Staying socially engaged has proven to be beneficial as well.

Giving your body what it needs. Your body wants to be healthy and heal. Take some time to get to know your own mind and body and provide it with the nutrients and exercise needed for your specific body and mind.

Take vitamins and supplements. This is a great daily habit. It is insurance for nutrients that may be lacking in your diet.

Resting when you need to. There is a big difference between resting and being lazy. You need to figure out how much rest you need as an individual and stick to that routine. Then it will be easier to tell if you're being swept into a lazy routine or if you actually need a rest. Many of us can use a power nap, or a short rest during the day in addition to a good night's sleep. So figure out how long you need to effectively recharge and then get back to doing something productive. Don't get trapped by your favorite streaming App!

Positive Affirmations for Health and Healing

"My body is healthy and full of energy."

"I only eat healthy food and give my body everything it needs to heal."

"I love getting exercise and always look for new enjoyable ways to exercise."

"I feel strong and fit."

"I listen to my body and give it what it needs."

"I feel healing energy all around me."

"The more I exercise, the more energy I get."

"I am only interested in things that serve my health."

"I forgive myself and others."

"I love my body and it serves me well."

"I am full of energy."

"I am in the process of healing."

"I allow myself to heal."

"I am creating inner peace."

"I am grateful for my body."

CHAPTER 6:

HABITS FOR LOVE AND MEANINGFUL HUMAN CONNECTION

What is love? This is the big question, there are even songs written about it. It is different for everyone. Primarily, most people think of love as attracting your soulmate and living happily ever after. This is a fantastic goal but it is just one small part of the love you need in your life. Love with a partner is very important, but so is self-love, career love and loving connections with others in your life.

The Ancient Greeks had 6 different words for 6 different kinds of love. Philia, (deep friendship), Ludus (playful love), Agape (love for everyone), Pragma (longstanding love), Philautia (love of the self) and Eros (sexual passion). And research has found that between all the world's languages there is a total of 14 different kinds of love! So if you're stalled in finding your soulmate, don't give up, but know that there are many kinds of love to fulfill feelings of loneliness, or the need for meaningful human connection.

In order to change your relationships for the better, you will have to change some of your habits. Many people believe that to create love in their life, they need to change their entire lifestyle, luckily, this isn't true. Here are some habit changes that will add up over time. Let's look at some destructive habits holding us back and see if we can replace them with some more positive productive ones.

Old Bad Habits

Not listening to others. Most people hear but don't listen. Some of the reasons why we don't listen are, our natural desire to talk, our instinct to judge others, you may have preconceptions or biases, your ego is getting in the way or you're just not interested and thinking about something else. Try to think about being respectful to everyone. Truly listening to them shows respect, whereas not paying attention or listening is disrespectful.

Focussing on the negatives. You may have friends that you mutually complain with, but for the most part, this is an unattractive quality when meeting new people and beginning new relationships of any kind. Try to be aware of your words. Instead of talking about some negative, destructive current event, find something positive and uplifting to talk about.

Talking and not doing. Many people are all talk and no action. Why? Because talking is easier than doing. Become aware of how much you talk and how much of it translates to action.

Not being open-minded. You may write off a wonderful person/ friendship or acquaintance because you have preconceived notions about them. Try to let their actions form your opinion about them. You might be surprised.

Pointing fingers and blaming others. This is a bad habit that many people do without being aware of it. When something goes wrong they quickly jump to blame or point a finger at someone else. Whether or not you are responsible for the problem, don't be quick to accuse others. Eventually, you can figure out why the thing happened, who is responsible and how to avoid it next time. But make sure you have the facts first before jumping to conclusions.

Not being vulnerable and putting yourself out there. Nobody wants to get their heart broken or be disappointed with friendships. This is a big deterrent for many people in seeking new relationships of any kind. A lot of it has to do with expectations. It is a great idea to make of list of the qualities you want to find in another person, but when you meet someone new don't expect them to be the person with all those qualities. You might need to meet a large number of people in order to find friends and partners that are compatible with you. Many times we think the first person we meet is "the one" when the chances of that being true are slim to none. Don't expect much from new acquaintances, take time to see if it is someone that fits and complements your lifestyle and goals for the future.

Judging others. Don't be quick to judge others, they might have other things going on in their lives than you can't readily see. You might lose out on a great relationship because you have created negative thoughts about them for no good reason. Try to be compassionate, when others do something that makes you raise your eyebrow, try to see their side of it as well.

New Good Habits

Visualizing your future. It's important to know exactly what you want in your life. What does your perfect life look like? Having money and a nice home or traveling around constantly with no responsibilities whatsoever? What kinds of relationships do you want to create in your life? The clearer your vision, the faster and more easily you can create an amazing life full of love. Download my free book "Creating a Vision Board" to help you get started.

Being a good listener. Listening is an art and a skill. Sometimes it's not easy, but it's worth working on because people will appreciate your efforts. So listen more than you speak. This quality makes you a lovable person, as it helps others feel seen and understood and makes them want to tell their story so they can be heard. This creates a fantastic feeling of connection between two individuals.

Being empathetic. It's not enough to be kind. We must understand and appreciate others as well. The more empathy one has with others' feelings, thoughts, or emotions, the better their ability to communicate difficult things. Try to walk in other's shoes, offer kindness to others and if you disagree about something, don't turn it into a debate.

Practicing mindfulness. It is easier to understand other people's perspectives when you're more present and aware of what is going on around you. Try looking at things from different angles. If this had happened to me, how would I have handled it? And "how would I feel if I were in their position? Being open-minded is very important when meeting new people. Your preconceptions or bias can get in the way and stop a fantastic friendship before it even gets started. Try not to judge or overreact when interacting with others.

Developing compassion. Sometimes it's not easy to find compassion in a world that seems to be full of negativity. However, by simply making a few small changes in how you think and act, you can become a more compassionate person. First, try to develop self-compassion and become more understanding and patient with yourself. Meditation might help, try to let all that judgment go out of you like an open window and then practice kindness towards others.

Never stop learning. Take some time for your hobbies and passions in life. Learning new things will help build up those happy brain cells which have an effect on our relationships. From how we act at our jobs to socializing with friends, learning new things will have a positive effect. Your brain will have more energy because it's engaged with what interests you and you will be interesting to talk to when meeting new people.

Treating everyone with respect. If you can take time out of your day to say "hello" as you pass by others, this will not only have a positive effect on you but also improve how they see themselves. Treating those around us with respect will ensure that good energy comes back to us as well. Treating people well will create smiles which can translate into love and happiness for all involved.

Listening to your instincts. Spend some time daily to get to know yourself and to listen to your inner voice. If you haven't been listening for a while, it will take some time before you hear it again. It will tell you all you need to know for your future dreams and goals and how to get there. Use Template 1 in Chapter 10 to get to know yourself and start listening to your inner voice and learn about your likes and dislikes. Eventually, your instincts will be spot on and you will trust them.

Loving yourself. You are all you have, so take care of yourself! Simply put, self-love is the assurance that your needs will be met and you will do whatever it takes to keep yourself healthy. Self-care means making sure all parts of oneself are taken care of, not just physical needs but also mental and emotional wellbeing as well.

Positive Affirmations for Love and Meaningful Human Connection

"I attract love from others because I love myself first."

"I radiate love to everyone I meet."

"I am a good person and am worthy of love."

"I am worthy of fulfilling relationships."

"I forgive myself for my past mistakes."

"I am grateful for the love I receive."

"I attract loving and trusting relationships."

"The Universe surrounds me with love."

"I love myself and others unconditionally."

"I find meaning and connection in many relationships."

"I practice listening and not speaking with everyone I meet."

CHAPTER 7:

HABITS FOR HAPPINESS

Happiness is different for everyone and it consists of all the topics in this book. It is the perfect blend, custom-made for your life. The things needed for your happiness are unique to only you. For some of us and at different stages in our life, sometimes we just don't know what would make us happy.

Use Template 1 in Chapter 10 to get an idea of what your subconscious true self is yearning for. If you have not yet made a vision board, get some magazines or newspapers, have a look through them and don't question what you are attracted to, just cut it out. It could be a new couch, a tranquil garden with a cup of tea, a sailing ship, a mountain, a forest, or a new car. Whatever you are attracted to cut it out and make an additional vision board if you have already made one. Keep it in a place where you can look at it multiple times throughout the day. Use the positive affirmations at the end of this chapter when you look at your vision board.

Good daily habits are the key to happiness. If we can identify what is causing the gloom and break those behavioral routines, you will be happier in your daily life.

Old Bad Habits

Procrastinating. Postponing or delaying a task or set of tasks is procrastination. Sometimes the longer you delay will cause negative consequences. This is a common habit that many people do without even knowing it. Make a to-do list and get to work now!

Not knowing yourself. How can you expect to find happiness if you don't know what makes you happy? Spend some time each day by yourself listening to your inner self and feeling what it is you want to accomplish in your life. Creating a vision board by going through magazines and cutting out photos of what you are attracted to, can help you learn what makes you happy. It can be a simple as a color that you enjoy and need more of in your home, it could be a new car or a new meaningful relationship. Spend some time setting some goals for achieving things that truly make you happy.

Not following your dreams. Dream big. After you have created your vision board of your big goals and the things that will truly bring you happiness, it's time to make a plan to get there. Using my book "365 days of Positive Affirmations", will help you reach your goals. Visualizations, affirmations, big goals and solid consistent plans to achieve them will ensure that you reach your dreams and live your best life.

Not setting goals. Many people go through life without any goals for the future. Please don't be one of them. We only have a short time on this earth to live up to our full potential. But it doesn't just happen. You need to set some goals and work at them to achieve the life you've dreamed of.

Not following your plan. It is worth it to spend some time making a solid plan to reach your goals. It can be a business plan or a list of affirmations and a vision board. After you've done all this hard work, don't stop! You are just getting started, many times people have great plans but they fail to follow through on them. Following your plan consistently and focussing will get you to your goals. Your plan is the yellow brick road to your dreams!

Holding grudges. I'll admit this is a tough one for me. If someone wrongs you or treats you badly, it is natural to respond by thinking of that person negatively and not wanting to be open with them again. Holding on to anger, bitterness and resentment has been shown to harm YOU and not just the person you direct your feelings towards. Rumination occurs when you think regularly about the person that wronged you and what occurred, this keeps us stuck and in a negative frame of mind. Harboring negative feelings is bad for you! If the person is important to you and has apologized, asked for forgiveness, and/or realized they have hurt you, then forgiving and accepting is a good option for you. If the person in question doesn't feel like they've done anything wrong, then your only option is to distance yourself from them "let it go", and get on with your life. If someone won't accept what they have done you can always thank them in your mind FOR GIVING you that experience and what you have learned from it and choose to minimally associate with that person. Try to forgive, but not forget. Move on with your life but don't give that person another chance to mistreat you.

New Good Habits

Maintaining your mental health. Happiness emanates from your mind. So, it's not just about what you do physically, but also mentally. Try to take care of how you feel inside and try to eliminate bad habits. You may think this sounds hard, but it takes only a few minutes per day. So set aside some time today to focus solely on improving your mood and developing a grateful, positive attitude.

Being grateful. Develop an attitude of gratitude. Being grateful for what you already have in your life will help attract more of what you want. You can use my Journal, "One Year of Gratitude Journaling" to help develop a grateful attitude and attract abundance into your life. Remember, when you have a grateful attitude you are living in grace, you will be attuned to the Universe and good things will continue to happen for you!

Getting to know yourself. This might be the ultimate key to happiness. Sadly, many of us become adults and don't know what makes us happy. It starts when you're young and you are unable to follow your dreams and the things that you enjoy. So that part of your inner voice gets turned off. Take some time each day to listen and cultivate your inner voice, it will tell you exactly what you need to be happy and fulfilled in your life!

Exercising regularly. You might think that exercise is just about the physical act of movement, but it's so much more than that. It can be mental, spiritual, and emotional as well! A little effort goes a long way, even if it's only 10 minutes at lunchtime or before bed each night. Exercise has been found to be beneficial in reducing symptoms of depression and boost happiness levels for some people. You could choose activities like running marathons or scaling cliffs. The trick isn't exercising until exhaustion sets in, but instead finding an activity that makes your heart sing without feeling overly challenging. Walking, a yoga class, a swim or a bike ride are all great activities to get started.

Accepting challenges and learning from them. Sometimes things come up that we didn't plan for, it is just a part of life. If you can see the silver lining in the clouds of challenge that arise, you will be able to learn something important and continue your journey to your goals that much wiser and more prepared for next time. When things go wrong, take care of yourself, try a deep breathing exercise, or spending some quality one-on-one time with friends/family members who love you. You can learn just as much from challenges and mistakes as you can from a success.

Facing stress. Stress is universal, and it can be a good thing. Stress helps us when we need to lift weights, for example. What matters most in life (and our health) is how one handles stressful events. Shifting your perspective on stressful issues will make them seem less daunting, and you might even find a bright side. Make a list of what needs to be done and go through the tasks one by one. A sense of humor can keep things light-hearted when needed as well. Positive affirmations like "I can manage everything" will help you feel less stressed when there is a lot that needs to be done.

Decluttering. Decluttering works like therapeutic medicine. For the next 20 minutes, can you set aside time to tidy up and pass some things on to others? Particularly, those areas in your home where things are all over and out-of-sorts. It takes only a few minutes a day to keep your home clutter-free. There are books written with tips and advice to help you as well.

Practicing mindfulness. Living in the present moment is a life-changing experience, and you can have the most happiness by being in the NOW. Try to go through the day without judging and/or overreacting to anything. Try to be mindful of where each day takes us, and trust that you are on your right path, regardless of what comes up. Walk, take breaks, share laughter or check mindfulness Apps.

Forgetting about your phone. The electronics world has been moving at a rapid pace, and it's easy to get caught up in that realm. Instead of sitting on social media scrolling through hours' worth of posts while eating, turn off your gadgets for at least an hour once a week and you'll be surprised by all the changes this makes. You can read, meditate or take a walk.

Smiling more. A study showed how smiling could make people happier, scowling - angrier and frowning - sadder. Smiling is good for your brain! When you smile, tiny molecules in our brains called neuropeptides are released, which helps fight off stress. Then other neurotransmitters like dopamine or serotonin come into play too! The best way to recover from a mental illness may be an easy smile. A recent study has found that forcing people who suffer from depression or anxiety disorders into smiling can provide them with some joy.

Meeting friends. If you're feeling lonely, reach out to your friends. A friend is the best remedy for a blue mood. It can feel like an uphill battle to make new friends and create meaningful relationships in adulthood, but that doesn't mean you should give up. Spend time with one or two people in particular whom you enjoy being around with nothing particularly exciting is happening. These friendships will remain strong because both parties care for each other when things aren't so busy. Friends of friends are also a fantastic way to meet new people.

Positive Affirmations for Happiness

"I am worthy of being happy."

"I accept myself unconditionally."

"I am proud of myself."

"I am creating the life I've always wanted."

"I allow myself to be happy now."

"I create my own happiness and joy."

"I expand my inner joy by sharing it with others."

"I have everything I need to be happy now."

"I am on the path to my goals and am enjoying the journey."

"I choose happiness."

"Everything is going to be ok."

"The timing in my life is perfect and everything is falling into place perfectly."

CHAPTER 8:

HABITS FOR SELF-CONFIDENCE AND SELF-ESTEEM

Self-confidence is a feeling about your own skills and abilities. Having self-confidence means you trust yourself and feel in control of your life. Self-esteem is an evaluation of your own worth. Self-esteem includes beliefs about yourself as well as emotional states and feelings. In order to build these in yourself, you first have to get to know yourself. You also need a record of making good choices for yourself. This is how your confidence and esteem will grow. Continuing with bad habits will lower your self-confidence and self-esteem while switching to some good and productive habits will increase these in yourself.

Old Bad Habits

Not knowing yourself. Spend some time each day getting to know YOU. This might sound odd since you might be a full-grown adult for many years now but trust me it's not. A huge number of people go through life not truly knowing their likes and dislikes and therefore can never be truly happy. Use the template in Chapter 10, to brainstorm some ideas about your likes and dislikes. By making choices based on your likes and dislikes, you will be happy with yourself and learn to trust yourself. Your self-confidence and self-esteem will grow and true happiness will find you.

Caring more about others than you do about yourself. This can mean pouring your energy into caring for others and not yourself, or it can mean caring about what others think about you more than your own feelings about yourself. Use affirmations to turn off the chatter in your brain, it only matters what you think about yourself. If you spend too much time caring for others, you might not have an option to stop immediately, but try to prioritize your own needs. Make time for yourself. Remember the famous airplane analogy, you have to put on your own oxygen mask before you can help others.

Not following your dreams. Many of us don't even have big dreams and goals. I encourage you to create a vision board and learn about yourself and your dreams for the future. Once you have identified them, you can make your plan and work every day on fulfilling your big dreams.

Caring about what others think. The need to be accepted is a strong human need. But sometimes it can become overwhelmming and consume our thoughts and actions. Quite often when this need becomes overwhelming it has to do with trauma from the past. If you grew up in an emotionally distant household, you might always be striving for comments about acceptance from others. There are also many other scenarios that can result in over-caring about what others think. Some ideas for overcoming this consuming need/bad habit are, to let go of perfection (however it turns out is just fine), get to know yourself more, find your tribe/like-minded people and become your own friend. Make a long list of positive affirmations and use them daily to help you get over this habit.

Feeling like others hold power over you. Some of us suffer from this bad habit and it is a perpetual loop. Often someone we care about can have a negative influence over some part of our life. To start combatting this feeling, you have to establish healthy boundaries and take responsibility for your own emotions, NOT theirs. It could be as simple as a friend always complaining to you and you don't want to hear about it anymore. Once you establish some boundaries with them, they may react in an uncomfortable way. This is their problem, not yours. Or your issue could be more serious, a spouse or parent that exerts a negative influence over you multiple times in a day. Try to spend more time away from this person and gradually set up boundaries. You may never be able to change this person but you can change yourself, and remember their reactions are about them, not you. Use deep breathing, positive self-talk and positive affirmations to help you get through.

Not being brave and courageous. Positive affirmations will help here. And doing a 180 to replace this habit of lacking courage. Tell yourself "I am brave, I am strong." over and over. Write it on your wall and set reminders on your smartphone. Bravery is a muscle, the more you do it, the easier it will get. Just imagine your self-esteem growing when you've done something courageous that you can be proud of.

Not trusting your instincts. If you are trapped in a negative relationship of any kind, you might not hear your own instincts anymore. But they are still there. Take a pencil and a paper or use the notes App on your smartphone, go for a walk and sit quietly somewhere. It will take some time to hear your instincts loudly, when you do, write them down so that you don't forget. Take action toward following your instincts.

Not doing what you said you would do. This is a habit that makes others think you can't be trusted but it also makes yourself think that you can't trust yourself. If you promise your body exercise and good food and then don't follow through, your inner voice and your actions are disconnected and you will never reach your goals. Not only that but you are undermining your instincts. Instincts get stronger when you act on them. Following through on your words shows yourself and others that you are a person of integrity and can be trusted.

New Good Habits

Following your dreams. If you have created a vision board of the things you would like for your future, now is the time to make some plans to get there! Your plan is the yellow brick road to your dreams and goals. Spend some time making a good solid plan and get to work every day until you reach each goal.

Spending quiet time with yourself. Learn your values and what is important to you. Meditating, going for a walk, drawing, knitting, exercising, or just sitting in nature will help you listen to your inner voice. Many people look to the outside world for all the answers to having a good life but the answers are inside you. Cultivate your inner voice, listening to it is a great daily habit.

Working on your bravery muscles. The more often you exhibit bravery and courage, the easier it will become. Visualize yourself being brave in certain difficult situations and use positive affirmations to help you develop your bravery and courage. "I am brave, I am courageous" are great daily affirmations.

Believing in yourself. Self-confidence is a powerful thing. It can propel you to accomplish your goals and dreams, or it could hold back all progress for fear of failure. Confident people aren't afraid of what will happen next in life because they have faith in themselves. Self-belief fuels their confidence which then sparks action even when faced with obstacles on the way. They trust themselves, maintain a positive outlook and talk positively to themselves.

Working on your determination. Self-confidence and self-esteem can be tough to build, but a big part of nurturing them is all in how we think. Having a positive, determined, unstoppable attitude about your dreams and goals, will ensure that you reach them. Use positive affirmations to develop your determination.

Don't let negative thoughts overpower you. An honest assessment of yourself and then taking action based on that awareness will go a long way. Stop preventing the things that you want by indulging in negative thoughts. Instead of thinking about all the people who have better lives than yours, focus on one thing at a time and do something new every day to make yourself feel better. Use positive affirmations to change your thoughts when negatives creep in.

Dressing immaculately. You know that feeling of success, self-confidence, and poise you get when your outfit is just right? Wearing nice clothes makes a person feel like they can take on anything. Not everyone needs to dress up expensively or in designer wear, but if you can make efforts with your own personal style it will help create balance in your life. It has been said that one's mood depends on how one looks. Fake it until you make it!

Talking slowly. We all have that friend who speaks too quickly. They're always in a hurry and don't care if you understand them or not. They're no fun when we try to chat because their words just fly by too fast. Try listening to some influential people. They talk slow and take their time. They make sure every word is important, no matter how small it is. Even if you don't feel confident speaking slowly, try to practice, your voice will sound more professional than if you rush. People will feel respected and you will be successful in your conversation.

Gaining more knowledge. It is important to become more knowledgeable in order for you to feel confident. This includes learning and researching business opportunities, which will help build your confidence in many different areas. You can learn about any topic or subject matter under the sun. But make sure it is something interesting to you. Use the internet or observe people around you. You can use books and magazines to get information that might not be online or in your local library. Educational institutions also offer classes that will help with any goal you have.

Maintaining good posture. Slouching is bad for you, but sitting up straight could help protect your brain and make it function better. When you slouch, your lungs can't do their job. They're compromised and don't get the oxygen they need to function at full capacity, which means less air for other parts of the body like our brain. But when we sit up straight it may help us think better as well because staying calm has benefits beyond just being more relaxed physically; this feeling helps with confidence too.

Following through on your words. If you don't intend to do something, then don't say you're going to do it. Don't be known as the person that is all talk and no action. Show yourself and others that "you mean what you say, and say what you mean."

Embracing discomfort. You must trust yourself and step outside of your comfort zone to raise self-esteem. Confident people didn't become so in a day. The bulk of people are stuck inside their own personal bubbles and think they'll achieve greatness without taking any risks. Remember your thoughts create your reality. So use affirmations like "I am successful", when stepping outside of your comfort zone.

Positive Affirmations for
Self-Confidence and Self-Esteem

"I believe in myself."

"I am proud of myself."

"I take steps every day to reach my ultimate dreams and goals."

"I make good choices."

"I am free."

"I am brave and courageous."

"I have big goals and work hard every day to achieve them."

"My skills and talents and valuable and will help me reach my goals."

"Every setback makes me wiser and stronger."

"How I feel about myself is most important."

"I deeply love and accept myself."

"I listen to my inner voice and trust what I hear."

"I can manage whatever comes my way."

"I am successful."

CHAPTER 9:

EXTREME HABITS: ADDICTIONS, SUBSTANCE USE, AND COMPULSIONS

If you suffer from one of these conditions, you will probably need professional help to stop them. Largely because these conditions cause your physical body to suffer, not only your mental health, and you will need multiple layers of support to successfully ditch these excessive habits that have turned into something else more serious. These conditions can start out harmlessly as a bad habit and quickly or slowly, over time turn into something that is out of control, harmful and can't be stopped by your willpower alone. Be sure to recognize if you need help and don't stop looking until you find it!

This book does not attempt to replace any medical or professional help, what it does is try to raise your awareness so that you can seek support if you need it.

Substance use and Addiction

Substance abuse is now commonly referred to as "substance use disorder" which is now a popular medical term for addiction. This encompasses both mild abuse and more severe dependence cases.

"Addiction" usually refers to someone's behavior while "dependence" refers to physical symptoms of withdrawal and tolerance. Substance use can become the main priority of an addicted person, regardless of the harm it causes themselves or others. Addiction is marked by changes in behavior caused by biochemical changes in the brain as a result of continued substance use.

If you are suffering from a serious addiction, it can be complicated to change it. In my opinion only, addiction problems can start as a deeply ingrained extreme bad habit that eventually causes serious mental and/or physical problems. It is not as easy as picking a new positive habit to replace it with. Most countries have a government website about addiction and substance use which is a good place to start looking for some extra help. Your medical doctor can give you some direction as well. You will need support on many levels and in some cases medical assistance to deal with physical withdrawal-type symptoms.

When someone becomes addicted it might likely stem back to missing an important part of human connection during one's developmental years. This tends to result in a big empty, missing piece in one's life that can easily be filled with drugs or alcohol or in other cases things like food. A good first step in recovery is analyzing why you may have started the addiction that you suffer from. What void and pain were you trying to pacify? If you can start to understand the motivations in starting, you can get some ideas as to which habits would be the most successful in helping to replace your addiction.

I have long believed that those individuals that seem to have a predisposition for substance use or addictions also have to greatest capacity to love and to accomplish great things. Their energy is misdirected. Often, the only new habit that can replace an addiction is meaningful human connection. Volunteering, doing community outreach, or seeking a job where you can help others might be some options to consider. There is also evidence that caring for animals, gardening and deep breathing can help to overcome substance use conditions. As I said earlier, this won't be as easy to fix as a habit like biting your nails, and you will need many layers of support.

Smoking can also fall under substance use, smoking starts as a bad habit, but quickly your body becomes dependant on the various chemicals involved in smoking and your brain becomes dependent on the routine as well. Some people can kick this habit on their own, but many require professional help and support. A medical doctor can prescribe medication to help with the craving and you can replace the smoking routine with exercise, deep-breathing, chewing gum, having a candy sucker or anything else that you come up with that will work for you personally.

Compulsions and Obsessive-Compulsive Disorder.

Obsessive-Compulsive disorder is a mental illness that causes people to have recurring, unwanted thoughts, ideas, or sensations (obsessions), that make them feel driven to do something repetitively (compulsions). How can you tell if your habit is normal or has OCD characteristics? People that have OCD sometimes have thoughts or actions that: take up over an hour a day, aren't enjoyable, are beyond their control, interfere with work or social life, or another part of their life. Some types of OCD are, "checking" things like locks, "contamination" (worry about dirt, etc) and symmetry and ordering (lining things up again and again). Stress can make OCD worse and there is no cure, but doctors recommend cognitive psychotherapy, medication, relaxation as well as some other useful treatments. If you think you suffer from this disorder, please find a professional to help you.

Problem gambling is a compulsive disorder and can be harmful to psychological and physical health. It is classified as an impulse control disorder and a gambling addiction can lead to feelings of helplessness and despondency and people that live with this disorder might experience depression, anxiety, and other problems. If you suffer from problem gambling please seek professional help to get you to stop this compulsive disorder.

Eating habits.

Some eating disorders can be created as a result of bad eating habits. But they usually have a psychological component as well. Seek help if you suffer from over-eating or under-eating. There is support out there, you just have to find it and not give up until you do! A medical doctor or a government website is a good place to start.

Positive Affirmations to overcome Extreme Habits

"I replace my bad habits with good ones that benefit my mind and body."

"I only put good nutrients into my body."

"I take one day at a time,

"I take care of myself."

"I comfort myself."

"I am becoming the best version of myself."

"I like the person that I am becoming."

"I am on the right path now and I will not stop."

"The past is over, the future is bright."

"I am becoming stronger every day."

"I am strong and fearless."

"My addiction is strong, but my willpower is stronger."

"I attract positive, healthful, and productive things into my life every day."

"Amazing things are headed my way."

"I have a plan to overcome my extreme habit and I stick to it."

CHAPTER 10:

TEMPLATES FOR HABIT CHANGING

If you have bought the paperback version of this book, you can write directly in the templates or photocopy them for future use. If you have the ebook version, you will have to copy them yourself onto a blank piece of paper. Use the templates over and over again to help you replace bad habits and create new ones so you can reach your goals and dreams quickly and effectively!

Template 1: Getting to know yourself

Use his template to brainstorm about yourself. Don't judge yourself just make a list as long as you can of your likes and dislikes. Awareness of yourself is a great first step in identifying which habits you want to change to help you on your journey to your big goals.

Template 2: Habits to Change list

Use this template to make a list of the habits that you want to change in your life. You can add to it at any time. Try to go through one at a time and make a plan to change your habit using the ideas in Chapter 3. You might want to avoid the cue or change the habit routine.

Template 3: Individual Bad habit awareness and progress

Once you have picked a habit to change, use this template to get to know your habit and the history of why you started. Make a plan to start changing your habit.

Template 4: Avoiding the Cue

If your bad habit can be stopped by avoiding the cue. Use this sheet. Brainstorm some ideas to stay away from your cue. Come up with some phrases to tell people if your habit has a social basis.

Template 5: Replacing the Routine.

If you can't avoid the cue for your bad habit, you will have to replace the behavioral routine. Find a new routine to replace the old destructive routine.

Template 6: More Rewards.

Use this template when you have a particularly bad habit routine that you have a hard time giving up. Make the list of rewards as long as you need to, add in things that have nothing to do with your habit to help motivate you. Remember if you can keep it up for 2-3 months, the new routine will become automatic.

Template 7: Slip-up Awareness

Slip-ups are part of life. Two steps forward and one step back. When you have a moment and do your old habit routine, use this sheet to analyze how it happened and how you were feeling. Make a plan to prevent another slip-up (but if it happens, it's ok, be patient with yourself).

Template 8: Bad Habit Daily Progress

Keep track of how many times per day you do your bad habit, and work on reducing the frequency.

Template 9: List of Good Habits to cultivate

Use this template for general good habits that don't need to replace any bad routines. Drinking more water, eating more fruit are things we should all cultivate and remind ourselves to do daily. If you are not replacing a bad habit, your new habit will take around 21 days to become automatic.

Template 10: Good Habit Daily Progress

Keep track of how many times per day you do your good habit, and work on increasing the frequency.

Template 1: Getting to know yourself

My likes (colors, people, places, things to do)

_____
_____
_____
_____
_____
_____
_____
_____
_____
_____
_____
_____

My dislikes (colors, people, places, things to do)

_____
_____
_____
_____
_____
_____
_____
_____
_____
_____
_____

Template 1: Getting to know yourself

My likes (colors, people, places, things to do)

_____

_____

_____

_____

_____

_____

_____

_____

_____

_____

_____

My dislikes (colors, people, places, things to do)

_____

_____

_____

_____

_____

_____

_____

_____

_____

Template 2: Habits to Change list

Bad Habits that I want to change:

_____

_____

_____

_____

_____

_____

_____

_____

_____

_____

_____

Phrase these Habits positively:

_____

_____

_____

_____

_____

_____

_____

_____

_____

_____

_____

Template 2: Habits to Change list

Bad Habits that I want to change:

_____

_____

_____

_____

_____

_____

_____

_____

_____

_____

_____

Phrase these Habits positively:

_____

_____

_____

_____

_____

_____

_____

_____

_____

_____

_____

Template 3:
Individual Bad Habit Awareness

Bad Habit that I want to change:

_____

_____

When did this habit start?

_____

_____

Who was I with?

_____

_____

How was I feeling?

_____

_____

Replacement routine ideas:

_____

_____

_____

_____

Positive Affirmations:

_____

_____

_____

_____

_____

_____

Template 3:
Individual Bad Habit Awareness

Bad Habit that I want to change:

_____

_____

When did this habit start?

_____

_____

Who was I with?

_____

_____

How was I feeling?

_____

_____

Replacement routine ideas:

_____

_____

_____

_____

_____

Positive Affirmations:

_____

_____

_____

_____

_____

_____

_____

Template 4: Avoiding the cue

Bad Habit that I want to change:

_____

_____

_____

_____

What is the cue or trigger?

_____

_____

_____

Time, place or person that is the cue/trigger:

_____

_____

_____

Ways to avoid the cue:

_____

_____

_____

_____

_____

Phrases to tell someone to avoid a social routine:

_____

_____

_____

_____

_____

Template 4: Avoiding the cue

Bad Habit that I want to change:

_____

_____

_____

_____

What is the cue or trigger?

_____

_____

_____

Time, place or person that is the cue/trigger:

_____

_____

_____

Ways to avoid the cue:

_____

_____

_____

_____

_____

Phrases to tell someone to avoid a social routine:

_____

_____

_____

_____

_____

_____

Template 5: Replacing the routine.

Bad Habit that I want to change:

_____
_____
_____
_____

What is the behavioral routine?

_____
_____
_____

Ideas to replace the routine:

_____
_____
_____
_____

Benefits of the new routine:

_____
_____
_____
_____
_____

Positive Affirmations to help with the new routine:

_____
_____
_____
_____
_____
_____

Template 5: Replacing the routine.

Bad Habit that I want to change:

_____

_____

_____

_____

What is the behavioral routine?

_____

_____

_____

Ideas to replace the routine:

_____

_____

_____

_____

Benefits of the new routine:

_____

_____

_____

_____

_____

Positive Affirmations to help with the new routine:

_____

_____

_____

_____

_____

_____

Template 6: More Rewards

Bad Habit that I want to change:

_____

_____

_____

_____

Phrase it postively:

_____

_____

_____

**Benefits of giving up the bad habit
and starting the new habit:**

_____

_____

_____

_____

_____

_____

More benefits/rewards for extra motivation:

_____

_____

_____

_____

_____

_____

_____

Template 6: More Rewards

Bad Habit that I want to change:

_____
_____
_____
_____

Phrase it postively:

_____
_____
_____

**Benefits of giving up the bad habit
and starting the new habit:**

_____
_____
_____
_____
_____
_____
_____

More benefits/rewards for extra motivation:

_____
_____
_____
_____
_____
_____
_____
_____

Template 7: Slip-up Awareness

What happened?

_____

_____

_____

Where was I?

_____

_____

_____

How was I feeling?

_____

_____

Who was I with?

_____

_____

What can I do next time to avoid a slip-up?

_____

_____

_____

_____

_____

Positive Affirmations to help staying on track:

_____

_____

_____

_____

_____

Template 7: Slip-up Awareness

What happened?

_____

_____

_____

Where was I?

_____

_____

_____

How was I feeling?

_____

_____

Who was I with?

_____

_____

What can I do next time to avoid a slip-up?

_____

_____

_____

_____

_____

Positive Affirmations to help staying on track:

_____

_____

_____

_____

_____

Template 8:
Individual Bad Habit Daily Progress

Bad Habit that I want to stop doing:

_____

_____

Date:	How many times per day:

Template 8:
Individual Bad Habit Daily Progress

Bad Habit that I want to stop doing:

_____

_____

Date:	How many times per day:

Template 9: List of
Daily Good Habits to cultivate

_____

_____

_____

_____

_____

_____

_____

_____

_____

_____

_____

_____

_____

_____

_____

_____

_____

_____

_____

_____

_____

_____

_____

_____

_____

_____

Template 9: List of
Daily Good Habits to cultivate

_____

_____

_____

_____

_____

_____

_____

_____

_____

_____

_____

_____

_____

_____

_____

_____

_____

_____

_____

_____

_____

_____

_____

_____

_____

_____

Template 10:
Individual Good Habit Daily Progress

Good Habit that I want to do more often:

_____

_____

Date: | **How many times per day:**

Template 10:
Individual Good Habit Daily Progress

Good Habit that I want to do more often:

_____

_____

Date:	How many times per day:

CONCLUSION

You can change your habits. And you don't have to be a psychology professor to do it either. In this book, we shared some little-known ways you can start changing your own behavior today, without the help of an expensive therapist or coach. Breaking old habits and creating new ones can be easier than you think. Remember, it takes around 21 days to form a new habit, but if you are breaking an old habit or replacing the old habit with a new one, it will take a bit longer, around 2-3 months.

It is possible to change your habits and create the life that you've always wanted! All you need is some determination, a written or visual plan and a couple of months of hard work. You can create the YOU that you've always known you could be. Just take it one step at a time, be patient, and believe in yourself. I know you can do it!

365 DAYS OF POSITIVE AFFIRMATIONS

A YEAR OF POWERFUL DAILY INSPIRATIONAL
THOUGHTS FOR CREATING CHANGE IN YOUR LIFE
AND ATTRACTING HEALTH, WEALTH, LOVE,
HAPPINESS, CONFIDENCE AND SELF-ESTEEM

NICOLE LOCKHART

1

AFFIRMATIONS AND GOAL SETTING

Why use Affirmations?

Affirmations are powerful ways to change your life. It is that simple. Basically, the proven principle of "like attracts like" is just as strong as gravity. It may be harder to explain, but that doesn't make it any less powerful. Do you wake up every morning excited and ready to take on the day? If you're like me this is not always as easy as it sounds. Positive affirmations are like snow tires in the blizzard of life.

Your brain is the original computer, it's the original smartphone and much more powerful. BUT, you have to realize that what you put in, or program, is what your brain will spit out. Really, it is just a machine, complicated with feelings and emotions. Lets take charge and put in some programming that will help us get out what we actually want out of life. Health, wealth, peace, financial prosperity, enjoyable relationships, it's all possible!

Affirmations should be spoken in the present tense as if they are happening right now or coming to you plain as day "Today, I will.." or "I am..". This makes your brain think these things are already here. So now your reality has no choice but to quickly catch up.

I encourage you to write down any affirmations that really speak to you, put them in your house where you can see them multiple times throughout the day. Use colors and even stickers to awaken your mind. Your mind will respond much stronger if colors or sparkles are added. Neurologists believe that stimulating yourself visually has a greater affect on putting your goals into action, compared to non-visual stimulus. You will need to make your desires as strong as possible, so that they are forced to become your reality.

This book is designed to be read daily, but it does not have to be. If you are feeling inspired, skip ahead and read some different affirmations, if you miss a day, no problem. This book can be used year over year, you can basically never get enough of these affirmations. The more you repeat them, the closer you will get to your goals, each year make a commitment to set some new goals, you can then use this book to transform your new yearly goals into reality. If you are feeling that you can't get enough affirmations, read as many as you like. The days are just a starting point to keep you on track and reading affirmations daily.

Goal Setting

Before beginning the daily affirmations, I would suggest setting out some clear goals for yourself. Then as you read each affirmation, you can apply it directly to one of your goals. I would recommend either writing down 4 or 5 master "BIG" goals and putting the list on your wall and/or creating a vision board, big or small. You can also put your list in your smartphone's notes if you are always on the go. If you are making a vision board with poster paper, get some magazines that interest you and go through them cutting out anything that you are attracted to without judging yourself. Glue the pictures to a poster paper, even one or two magazine pictures of really important things taped to you bathroom mirror are better than nothing.

Some goals might be:

- I find a new, enjoyable and lucrative career I meet my soulmate
- I help my body become healthy and fit I buy a new car
- I buy my own house
- I earn an extra $1,000 before the end of the year

Written goals should have some or all of these qualities:

- Specific
- Measurable
- Achievable
- Realistic
- Time-bound

This is known as the S.M.A.R.T. acronym for goal setting.

Now that you have determined exactly what you want, you need to state how you will do it. If your goal is to be healthy, write out a plan statement such as:

Goal: To become healthy and fit

Plan: and I will accomplish this by eating less sugar and exercising every day.

Goal: To earn $10,000 extra this year

Plan: and I will accomplish this by selling 100 wooden tables that I have made.

As much as we would like to think our goals will magically manifest themselves, with zero effort on our part, that is just not the case. This is both good news and bad news. The good news is that change will only come to people that desire it and the not so good news is you actually have to make an effort to start the process. If you desire wealth, the only way to real fortune is to provide a service or sell something of value to others. This doesn't mean you have to slave away extra hard to earn extra money. Look at the most financially successful people, most of them have their businesses set up very well, so that they can sit back and enjoy themselves. You can have this as well, think about new ways to serve people. There are ways to leverage yourself so that the amount of work you do is minimal compared to the reward. You just need to be open to some new ideas.

Don't worry if you don't yet have a plan for all of your big goals. Maybe you want to buy your own house and need $100,000 for a down payment. It might take a while to come up with a viable plan. Keep this in mind as you do your daily affirmations and manifest yourself a good solid plan. Plans for big goals can take time to uncover, be patient.

In addition to consciously manifesting the goals on your list or poster board, there is a huge unconscious, unexplainable power at work as well. I have a personal story, in my 20's, my cat had passed away, I wasn't even looking for a new kitten but my friend had brought me one as a gift. It was the cutest, fluffiest, little orange male kitten. I kept him and he was my cat for many years. When he was about a year old I took another look at an old poster board I had made years before receiving the kitten. As I was looking through the pictures of houses and tropical destinations. I found glued in the corner, a tiny picture I had cut out of a fluffy orange kitten. Be warned, when you start listing your goals and start taking steps to manifesting them, powerful energy is involved. Like a magnet being turned on, these goals are slowing moving closer to you. Visual stimulation, adds another level of incredible power to your brain.

In addition to your big goals, I would also suggest a list of some daily attainable goals as well, for example:

- eat less sugar
- get more exercise p
- practice patience
- go to bed on time

These will help you feel good on a daily basis, so that you can focus and use your energy to achieve your big goals.

So let's begin!

I

DAILY AFFIRMATIONS

January 1

"Today, I will let go of things and people that I no longer need in my life."

Maybe you need to move out some old furniture and make a new workspace or distance yourself from unsupportive people in your life. Let them go with peace and make room to embrace the new things that are coming into your life.

January 2

"I welcome and embrace change."

Change is uncomfortable, I don't think there is any way around that. Anything new will feel different, but when it's a positive change, it doesn't take long to enjoy it. Letting go of the old and letting in the new can feel strange, trust that it is the right thing to do, keep moving forward, you will begin to enjoy the change soon.

January 3

"I will create prosperity and abundance in my life by providing services or products to people that need them."

If you are wanting to increase your bank account, remember true wealth, can only come to you in return for a service or product. What can you offer other people?

January 4

"Today, I welcome all new opportunities."

When opportunity knocks, be ready. Opportunity only knocks once so get ready for when it arrives. Some people say opportunity looks a lot like work, so be ready to work hard when a golden opportunity presents itself.

January 5

"I will listen to my body today."

Do you need more sleep, more energy, or more time to yourself? Try to find a quiet space to think about what your body needs for a successful year ahead.

January 6

"Positive, supportive people are drawn to me."

Regardless of your goals, you will likely need a team. Once, you start your journey, you will meet the people that you need to help you along your path. By being positive and supportive yourself, people with these qualities will be drawn to you.

January 7

"My ideas are valuable."

Dig deep inside yourself. What idea have you had in the past that you haven't acted on? Maybe you quickly thought "that was a bad idea, it will never work". Yet the idea has never left you, give it a chance. Use affirmations to knock out the doubt.

January 8

"I possess the ability to make smart decisions for myself."

Even if you feel like some of your decisions have not worked out for the best, it's never too late to make some decisions from your heart. Listen quietly to what your heart is wanting for your future.

January 9

"I trust the journey that is bringing me to my goals."

Once you have set some goals, your path to them is also set, and it doesn't always make sense. Sometimes we have to get rid of old baggage or things that are no longer useful in our lives before we can start the productive part of our journey. Know that your journey is right on course.

January 10

"I have a solid plan to reach my goals, and I'm sticking to it!"

Persistence will get you there! Remember, if you are still waiting to uncover your plan, by repeating this, it will come to light soon, be patient. Try to think outside of the box, do some brainstorming to help find a clear, viable plan.

January 11

"My self-confidence is increasing, I am proud of myself."

Me, myself and I. It was you at the start of your life and it will be you and yourself at the end. Once you have committed to making changes in your life, you will begin to trust yourself. You will be the pillar of strength that you have always needed.

January 12

"I design my life and I am taking charge."

Nobody else is going to do it for you. Maybe it's time to step it up, more goals, more affirmations and more trust in your journey that is bringing you closer to your goals.

January 13

"I have all that I need to make today a productive and successful day."

What resources do you have at your disposal? If you aren't clear on specific work for today, do some behind the scenes work. Market research for a new project or reading about health. If you choose to have a day of rest, consider this to also be a success.

January 14

"Money comes quickly and easily into my life."

This is one of my favourites, if you desire more financial gain, write this affirmation everywhere to remind yourself to repeat it.

January 15

"I am persistent in whatever I do."

Slow and steady wins the race. Pace yourself, you don't need to do everything all at once. Persistence pays, think of the children's story "The Tortoise and the Hare", persist and persevere and rest as well.

January 16

"I believe in myself."

If you don't who will? Repeat this if doubt is creeping in, and remind yourself that you have your back and you will support yourself through everything that comes up.

January 17

"My confidence is increasing, I have much to offer the world."

You, yes you, are an important part of this world. Every unique individual has something amazing to offer. Think about drawing a picture or writing a poem. This is just a physical example of something you can make that could be around for hundreds of years.

January 18

"I can do anything I put my mind to."

Whatever goals you have chosen, if they exist on this earth, you can accomplish them. Be patient, bigger goals might take longer and require more extreme plans and preparation.

January 19

"Today, I am thankful for everything in my life."

Take a look around, you likely have a roof over your head and food in the fridge. You have a lot to be thankful for, thankfulness and gratitude open the gates to fulfilling your goals.

January 20

"I rely on myself."

You might be a young adult wanting to be more independent or perhaps you feel trapped in your job or current relationship. You have the power to get yourself out of any situation, and become self-reliant.

January 21

"I choose to be kind to everyone that I encounter."

A little kindness goes a long way. Do your best to exude kindness to everyone you meet, kindness is a quality that comes back to you exponentially. It doesn't cost anything and is very powerful.

January 22

"I am discovering interesting and exciting new paths each and every day."

The world is full of endless possibilities, when we get caught up on the hamster wheel of daily life, it is hard to see them. Today, take a different route to work or to check your mail. Look around at all the opportunities that are close by.

January 23

"I am wise."

See the world for what it is. No need to protect people or sugar coat things. With each experience you have, your judgment will improve. Take some time to think about the situation before you reach a conclusion or speak about it.

January 24

"I am proud of myself."

Others may not agree with your choices, so you need to be your own champion. Be proud of the progress you have made so far. As you uncover your strengths and continue to put them into practice, your confidence will increase.

January 25

"I am courageous and will never back down from what I believe in."

Always do what you know to be right. Don't be bullied or pushed around by people with their own agenda. This includes your plans to your goals, believe in them and don't ever stop.

January 26

"I desire wealth."

In order for wealth to come to you, you need to make your desire extremely strong. Think of how it would feel to have all the wealth you dream of. Add to your vision board or make a cut out with the number of dollars you wish to acquire. Make it colourful and sparkly, this will put your brain in overdrive attraction mode.

January 27

"I am getting on with my life."

Sometimes we feel held back by certain people or circumstances in our lives. Repeating this will help those blockages fade away. Put on those snow tires and get going with your own life!

January 28

"I am worthy of a healthy body."

Having a healthy body is important for enjoying the goals you have worked so hard for. Make a decision to be more aware of what you are putting into your body.

January 29

"I am patient."

Good things come to those who wait. This doesn't mean just sit around and do nothing. Good things come to those who are persistent and patient. Let's be real, a new job or car could take months to procure, a new house could take a year or more to achieve or your soulmate could show up at anytime. They will come when you are ready to receive them. Trust that it is all working perfectly.

January 30

"I choose to be peaceful."

You can be strong and brave and still choose peace, you don't need to fight with others to be successful. Just carry on your path and most problems will resolve themselves.

January 31

"I am planting the seeds in my mind today for my ultimate future."

We reap what we sow. Now is the time to sow seeds for the future. Change doesn't happen overnight, but planting seeds now, and nurturing them, will give you the results you have been dreaming of.

2

February 1

"I am creating the life I want and I am enjoying it now."

Take some time today to do something out of the ordinary for yourself. Get your favourite expensive coffee drink, or buy a piece of clothing that brings a smile to your face.

February 2

"I am open to new ways of improving my health."

Maybe it's time to order some new vitamins or try the new juice bar down the street. Maybe you've been thinking about changing your diet or incorporating more exercise into your day. Get creative, find some new and fun ways to improve your health.

February 3

"I am creating all the success and prosperity I desire."

Gather some magazines or newspapers, cut out pictures that speak to you, a new car, a new house, a pet, a picture of a relationship you would like to pursue or even a picture of a coffee cup that you are visually attracted to. Glue them to a poster board or tape them to your wall if you don't have glue. Surround yourself with pictures of your future. If you have already made a vision board, you can add to it anytime.

February 4

"I am brave and I am creating positive change in my life."

Baby steps, the beginning of anything is always the hardest. When doubt and despair creep in, be armed with some good affirmations that speak to you, so you can reprogram your brain.

February 5

"I am proud of my actions."

Others may not agree with your choices and actions, especially if they can't see where all your new plans are headed. What you think of yourself is all that matters. Choose your actions carefully, and be incredibly proud of yourself.

February 6

"I will celebrate this day with gratitude and joy."

Whatever this day brings, be grateful. Gratitude opens the floodgates to unlimited potential in all areas of your life. Being gracious will help you exude joy, try to spread some joy to others.

February 7

"Today I stay in my lane, and don't compare myself to others."

Think of horses running a race, they all have blinders on so that they stay in their lane and don't look at what their neighbours are doing, blinders are the only way a horserace will work. Try to put some blinders on, and think only of your own goals. Everybody has their own set of challenges and you don't need to concern yourself with their progress.

February 8

"I am finding ways to afford the things I need and want."

Instead of compromising your needs and wants, find ways to accomplish them. Be open to new opportunities to create wealth. Making a vision board will help find a means to your goals.

February 9

"I am feeling happy and successful and feel grateful for my life."

Even if you're not feeling happy and successful today, this affirmations will attract happiness and success, "like attracts like". By saying this you are resonating with happiness and success and bringing more of them into your life.

February 10

"I love my body shape, it is perfect and the way it is intended to be."

Although we can not change our body's shape or height, we can change what we put into it. Try to eat some more fresh fruits and vegetables, your body will thank you!

February 11

"I have faith in my abilities to achieve my goals."

Once you learn what your passions are, you will be aligned with your purpose. You will see that your abilities actually match, and are designed to reach your goals.

February 12

"I am learning new things that will result in bringing me happiness, freedom, and purpose."

You will have to learn some new things. The first of which is reprogramming your brain with affirmations. Then you may have to learn new skills for your new job or some new daily routines that will contribute to your physical health.

February 13

"I trust myself, I am confident that I am doing the right thing."

Which comes first, trust or confidence? They go hand in hand, the more you trust yourself, the more confident you can be, and the more confident you are, the more your self- trust will grow. As you continue to manifest change, both will increase.

February 14

"I attract real love into my life."

Real love is doing things for others, because you know it is important to them or it is something they enjoy, and expecting nothing in return. Pay it forward at the drive through or do something for a family member that is needed and appreciated. This will be reciprocated in ways we can't imagine.

February 15

"I am free."

If you are wanting change in your life, chances are you are feeling trapped in one or more areas of your life. While you are enduring your present situation, know that you really are free, you are just disposing of residual garbage, which can take time. Go for a walk outside, feel the sun and the wind on your face. You are free.

February 16

"I am consistently becoming more successful."

Success can occur in any area of your life. By focussing on affirmations daily, writing some of your favourites in a visible place, and making a vision board for the areas of your life that you want to change, these things are forced to come closer to you.

February 17

"I release all negativity."

It is easy to get in the habit of cursing at slow drivers or being easily annoyed for whatever reason. Let these negative feelings pass through you, there is no need to react or hold on to them.

February 18

"I have a lot to offer the world and receive fulfillment in return."

There are times when we feel insignificant, like the world would continue regardless of what we do. This is doubt and despair creeping in, pick your favourite affirmations to fight and get ready to provide a service or product to people that need them, you will be rewarded in return.

February 19

"This morning, I wake up ready for a new day of exciting possibilities."

Be open to new things, if someone strikes up a conversation while you are waiting in a lineup, listen to what they have to say. You might just stumble upon some unexpected inspiration.

February 20

"Today, I will endure."

Some things just need to run their course. Maybe you are wanting to create a new career or find a new place to live. While you are manifesting this into your life, you still have to attend your old job. Endurance is an incredible quality to posses. Know that enduring your present situation is bringing you closer to your goals.

February 21

"I am worthy of joy in my life."

Maybe it's been awhile since you have delighted with glee. As an adult, these opportunities are few and far between, observe some kids playing, or go to a park and watch the wildlife playing around. You will be reminded that joy is one of the simplest emotions.

February 22

"I always attract only the best positive people into my life."

If you repeat this today, and any other day, you will find you have nothing in common with negative people. Unsupportive people that are judging you or enjoy watching other people fail will fade away and disappear out of your life.

February 23

"I will make impressive contributions to the world today."

Whether it's going to work and doing your job, drawing a picture, or making an invention. Know that whatever it is, it is valuable to the world. Without your efforts the world would just be rocks and trees, know that whatever you have done today is important.

February 24

"I am always creating and looking for new opportunities."

If you don't see a new opportunity in front of you right now, then make one! With your goals in mind, go to a bookstore or look online for a new topic that interests you.

February 25

"I am not afraid of making mistakes."

Actually there are no such things as mistakes. Maybe you regret a certain choice you made. This regret will make sure it never happens again. Look at the "mistake" as a learning opportunity, one you have now learned and never have to experience again.

February 26

"I am calm and content."

Remember to breath deeply, oxygen is life, it will calm us and heal us. If you are feeling exasperated, take some time to practice deep breathing.

February 27

"I choose to only let positive thoughts into my mind."

You brain is the original computer, input results in output. Choose thoughts that will get you where you want to be. If I feel doubt or despair creeping in, I go straight to repeating affirmations. It is a good idea to have a few favourites written on the wall or saved in your smartphone for doubting emergencies.

February 28

"My needs and wants are important to me."

They may not be important to others, so don't fool yourself into thinking others really care about what makes your heart happy. They are often too busy thinking about their own path. Only you are responsible for fulfilling your wants and needs.

February 29

"Practicing gratitude brings me joy."

Reflect on the things that you are thankful for. Buy some thank you cards to have on hand to give to people to show your gratitude.

3

March 1

"I love the way I look."

Accepting and loving the way you look is essential for happiness. The things that you were born with and can not change, make you - you. But there are some things you can change, how about a new haircut or colour, or some new clothes?

March 2

"I am focused on my work and welcome new work opportunities."

Think about some other ways you can provide the service or product that you specialize in. There may be other income streams just waiting for you to tap into them.

March 3

"I have everything I need to face any challenges that arise."

Challenges always have a way of popping up, when we view them as an opportunity for learning, we have the ability to make them disappear forever. It is the challenge that is overlooked that continues to show up.

March 4

"I am living my life with purpose."

Doing meaningful work will harmonize with the forces that will bring you what you are wanting to achieve. Whether it is your full-time job that is meaningful to your soul, or your hobby, do more of it.

March 5

"My relationships are healthy."

By making this affirmation a part of your inner programming, unhealthy relationships will fade away. There will no longer be an unhealthy connection to keep them going.

March 6

"Today, I will have success."

Keep an eye open for even small successes, maybe you remembered to put less sugar in your coffee or made a healthy choice for a snack. However small, these are important successes.

March 7

"Today, I focus on positive progress."

Take a minute to pat yourself on the back, you have already come so far. The beginning is the hardest and you will soon see the fruits of your labour.

March 8

"I am creating my destiny."

You are the captain of your own ship. Set your goals and get ready to achieve them! Don't settle for anything less and do your best to block out negative people.

March 9

"Today, I let go of fear forever."

As you become more self-reliant, fear will disappear, know that you will always be there for yourself, and you can get through anything that comes your way.

March 10

"I abandon old habits that no longer serve me."

Do you need to stop some bad habits? Replacing them with something positive is the best way to leave them far behind. For example, if you have a donut everyday for breakfast, find a fruit or a sugar free treat that you can eat instead of the donut.

March 11

"I breathe good energy in and breathe bad energy out."

This might take a while to get right because you are focussing on breathing and thinking at the same time. Find a quiet space and give it a try.

March 12

"I'm in charge of creating my path in life."

Parents are the worst for pushing their hopes and dreams onto their children. We are each born with unique skills and gifts, you are still probably figuring out your own. So don't let anyone else tell you what you should or should not be doing.

March 13

"I will be patient with myself while I heal."

Maybe there is a part of your past that still presents itself today, a limiting belief or a childhood tragedy. Look for ways to heal, take your time, and treat yourself with love and patience.

March 14

"I earn money doing what I love."

Even if you have a job that you don't especially like, start up a side gig that you love. It doesn't matter how big or small. Once you start, you will be helped along your way.

March 15

"I attract success and happiness."

That's right, your new energy is attracting success and happiness right now, can you feel it? Do something for yourself today, a walk at your favourite park or dig out some old songs that remind you of how far you have come.

March 16

"I am creating a healthy body by talking about and thinking about my wellness."

The six best doctors in the world are sunlight, rest, exercise, diet, self-confidence and friends." ~Steve Jobs

March 17

"I can feel happiness even though I am alone."

Maybe you are still searching for your soulmate or even just a kindred spirit. Remember, a cup of tea and a good book are a close second. Take care of yourself, order your favourite dinner, put on your favourite movie and have an enjoyable evening for one.

March 18

"I receive unexpected opportunities."

Networking with supportive people and taking risks will help you create meaningful opportunity in your life. Sometimes opportunities look like a lot of work, don't pass them up because of this. If an opportunity is in front of you, grab it!

March 19

"I let go of what I can not change."

Have you been holding on to the hope that someone or something will change? Chances are, if it hasn't happened yet, it may never will, time to let go and move on with your own goals.

March 20

"I am ready to begin my journey to my goals."

Not going all the way and not starting are two mistakes people make in their lives. One step in front of the other. Slowly but surely you will get there.

March 21

"I am grateful to be alive."

We are all so lucky to be living right now, it's the best time in history of mankind. Be grateful that you are alive now and take care of your body so it will last a long time.

March 22

"I have valuable talents and skills."

Do you have untapped skills or talents that have never realized their full potential? Maybe you really enjoyed woodworking in high school, or baking. These are just some great of examples of modern day side gigs, and many times they can become a full time job.

March 23

"I teach others to believe in me because I believe in myself."

If you have doubters in your life, remember living well is the best revenge. We don't need to be vengeful at all, but stop worrying about what others think, their thoughts about you will only change when they actually see change within yourself. Focus on yourself.

March 24

"I am feeling confident and strong today."

This affirmation is a protective one, hopefully by now you are feeling more strong and confident in general. By repeating this, you are shutting out doubt and despair, which are just waiting for a chance to creep into your mind.

March 25

"My past is not an indication of my future."

You have chosen to make changes in your life, don't get stuck remembering things that have held you back in the past, the past is over, while you may have to come to terms with events that occurred, do not let these events limit your future. I tell myself "next time, I will do it differently" if a past choice continues to bother me.

March 26

"I am at peace with myself."

Do you suffer from an inner struggle? Something that you know isn't good for you but you just can't stop doing it? Take a step back and try to view yourself from a distance. What could you tell yourself to encourage positive change? There are also apps for changing habits that many people find helpful.

March 27

"The decisions I make help bring me closer to my goals."

Trust that you are making the right decisions, sometimes it might look like you are completely detouring the right path to your goals.

Making decisions from your heart will always move you in the right direction.

March 28

"Today, I will forgive."

Although I am a firm believer in only forgiving those who have asked for forgiveness. If they haven't accepted that they did something wrong and hurt you why give them your forgiveness? But there is something else you can do, you can thank them FOR GIVING you that experience. There are some people that you simply can not trust, but thanking them for the experience melts away any resentment you are carrying.

March 29

"I can do it all."

Do you ever have moments where you feel overwhelmed? For me, I usually wake up early morning worrying and thinking about all the things on my to-do list. Repeat this affirmation, there is no need to worry, you can do it all. One thing at a time.

March 30

"I am in charge of my life."

If you are part of a family or work group that sees you as a part of the whole, it can be difficult to do what is best for you. Perhaps you can find a way to forge your path while still being a part of the group, but if not, consider being brave and venturing off on your own.

March 31

"I am excited for the future."

Feel excited, act excited, talk excitedly, enthusiasm and excitement are contagious. An excited state of mind will be one of your super powers to help you reach your goals.

April 1

"Every day is becoming easier, I am getting closer to my goals."

Have faith, it will all come together. One step at a time. Think of climbing a long winding staircase, you can't see the top, but each step brings you closer. Know that you are on your way and try to enjoy the journey.

April 2

"Difficulties make me stronger."

Do you ever have days where things just seem to go wrong? You forgot your password, your bank card is not working or you dropped and spilled something by accident? Stay calm, these things will only make you stronger. Maybe you need to put in place some backups to ensure these things don't happen again.

April 3

"I deeply love and accept myself."

This affirmation is used in EFT (Emotional Freedom Technique), which is a whole other topic all together. Self- love and self-acceptance are key to healing and moving on. You need to know that you have your own back. Know that you are there for yourself and you can conquer almost any challenge.

April 4

"Today, I give extra care and love to the parts of me that need it."

Whether you are suffering from aches and pains or something more serious. Focus on the part of you that needs extra care. Be open to new ways of creating health and eliminating sickness in your body.

April 5

"I make smart decisions."

Have faith in yourself. The decisions you make are based on your experiences and what you think is best. Even if your choice doesn't turn out how you had hoped, you will still learn something, making you smarter. Next time do it differently.

April 6

"I'm in charge of how I react to others."

When we are cultivating peace and positivity in our lives, we can sometimes run into people that find it necessary to be difficult. Acknowledge that you are no longer playing that game, excuse yourself to go do something important or tell them you will have to call them back later.

April 7

"Each day is becoming easier."

You have been committed to change now for awhile. Although there may be some rough days in the beginning while your present situation is aligning with your future goals, once this passes, every day will be easier.

April 8

"I am creating change."

That is what this is all about, creating change and you are doing it now, affirmations and goals will set you in motion for change.

April 9

"I follow my bliss."

It's true that sometimes we have to do things we don't especially like doing. Going to the dentist or paying taxes. These things will seem much more insignificant if you can identify your true bliss and passions. Look around, what colours do you like to see? Do you enjoy plants in your home? Or maybe go shopping for a new framed feature picture for your living room. Whatever inspires you, do more of that.

April 10

"I appreciate everything I have in my life."

Gratitude, is the essence of fulfillment. Appreciating and being grateful for everything in your life, even if it's something you need to let go of, will pave the way to fulfilling your dreams and goals.

April 11

"I desire health."

Do you take steps everyday to ensure your body remains healthy? Without health, it is difficult to accomplish anything. Make a commitment to yourself to spend a certain amount of time devoted to your health. Whether you want more energy or you feel fine, don't let this slip, it is one of the most important things.

April 12

"Today, I will watch for a sign, something calling me to investigate further."

It could be an old song on the radio or an add on a billboard, look for something that resonates with you, this will help guide you for the year ahead.

April 13

"Today, great things are coming to me."

Try to focus on the wonderful small things that come into your life today. A cup of coffee or a phone call from a friend.

Being gracious for the small things will open the door to bigger things.

April 14

"I rely on myself."

Have you ever felt like your hands are tied because you have to rely on someone else? Like you can't make the choice you want to because you need to make someone else happy? If one of your goals is independence and self-reliance, quietly hatch your plan, before you know it you will be able to assert your own needs and wants.

April 15

"I welcome new opportunities into my life."

Try to be open to new business ventures and new ways to make friends or meet people. You can still be smart and safe while exploring new opportunities.

April 16

"I believe the universe is giving me exactly what I need, when I need it."

Once you have made your plan for reaching your goals, and have made it clear how you will work towards getting there, the universe will conspire to make sure you succeed. We can't always see how or why things are happening, but trust it is unfolding perfectly.

April 17

"The small steps I make will get me to my goals."

If it seems to be slow going, be persistent, you will achieve your goals. Focus, patience and persistence will get you there. It is the small pieces that will make the big picture.

April 18

"I am feeling energetic today."

Start the day with some stretches and deep breathes of fresh air. Try to drink more water and only drink coffee in the morning. Make choices to eat food that gives you pure energy instead of slowing you down.

April 19

"I am strong and brave, I have the courage to face my fears."

You can do it! Many of us have a voice telling us that we can't achieve a certain success, repeating these words will help drown out that voice and build your courage.

April 20

"I will not let anyone or anything stop me from pursuing my goals."

Don't be distracted by nearby pitfalls, focus your energy on your own path. If challenges arise along your journey, deal with them. Be aware of the difference between your challenges and the challenges others face.

April 21

"Today, I promise to listen to my needs."

Try to listen quietly to uncover what your heart and soul are yearning for. It is hard to listen with the daily hustle and bustle, but try to take a few minutes to sit outdoors in a park or a forest. Find somewhere quiet without distractions, close your eyes and listen quietly to the thoughts that enter your mind. Bring a pen and a paper to note these golden ideas.

April 22

"I am choosing to make changes in my life and reach my goals."

If you always do what you've always done, you will stay right where you are. Congratulations for deciding to make changes and get the life you've always wanted.

April 23

"Today, I am looking for new ideas that inspire me."

Take some time to shop online or go to a store and just look around. Don't judge, just see what your eyes are drawn to.

April 24

"Today, I release any negative beliefs I have about attracting money."

Thoughts like "money is scarce" or "you need to hold on to money" are just not true. There is enough money for everyone. Money is just a physical representation of how you contribute to society, what product or service can you offer? And who can you help with extra money that has already come to you?

April 25

"I am courageous and I believe in myself."

You have the ability to do whatever you set your mind to. Stand tall and face your fears, nobody else will do it for you. Push through, your goals are waiting for you.

April 26

"Change comes at the right time."

We don't know how change will unfold in our lives. Often we have to set into motion our plans for reaching our goals and then eliminate things that are holding us back. Once we actually see some results it is very exciting! Be patient if it hasn't happened yet.

April 27

"I embrace every season of my life."

You may feel like you want to fast forward through certain parts of your life. Try to enjoy every part, each one is setting the stage for future, more gainful seasons. Could Spring arrive without Winter?

April 28

"I am persistent in making my dreams reality."

Persistence is continuous positive action in spite of difficulties. Keep your eye on the prize.

April 29

"I will not make excuses for anything."

Too cold to walk to work, too tired? Healthy food is too expensive? Throw out those excuses and just do it. Excuses will keep you stuck forever.

April 30

"I love and appreciate my body."

You only get one body. Learn to love and appreciate it regardless of its shortfalls, problems or limitations. Make the best of the body you were given and take care of it.

May 1

"I am open to new ideas that will contribute to my success."

Once you've set some goals for yourself, either written goals or on a vision board, the next step is working on your plan to achieving them. You never know where new ideas might come from, so be open to new ideas that you previously had never considered.

May 2

"I appreciate my efforts."

In the beginning especially, it can seem like all work and no results. Thank yourself for all that you do. Buy yourself something, or do something for yourself that you enjoy, to thank yourself for all your hard work so far.

May 3

"I love to exercise."

Even if you don't, repeating this will help change your mindset. Look into some new forms of exercise that you enjoy. Yoga, a hike or swimming perhaps.

May 4

"I am working towards financial freedom."

Work on your budget, pay off your credit cards and try to save a little bit each month. Work on your BIG goals and remember to give some money to those in need when extra money starts coming in.

May 5

"My curses are actually my blessings."

Is there something you have viewed negatively about your life? Maybe you were born with a disability or a learning challenge. Since you are an expert in living with this challenge why not try to help others? You could write a book or support people that need it.

May 6

"I attract positive people into my life."

Be the positive person that you want to attract. Focus on the good in your life and comment on others successes. Be gracious and talk to yourself in a positive way.

May 7

"I know I will reach my goals."

Maybe you still have in the back of your mind "maybe I will and maybe I won't". Put an end to that now. Make a commitment that you WILL reach your goals.

May 8

"I am creating positive changes in my life."

In addition to you master goal list, I would suggest creating a daily one as well. Daily goals could be more exercise or eating less sugar. Replacing unhealthy things with something better, is the best way to change your habits.

May 9

"I approve of my choices."

It's your life. No one has to live with your choices except you. You will find there are many people who will want to put in their two cents about what choice you should make. Thank them for their concern and then do what you choose.

May 10

"My sleep is relaxing and refreshing."

Some tips for sleeping better are: staying up a bit later so that when you fall asleep it will be a deeper sleep, avoid napping, only drink coffee in the morning and look into supplements like melatonin if you still have trouble sleeping.

May 11

"Each day, I put my plan into action to consistently work towards my goals."

Rome wasn't built in a day, be patient with yourself. As long as you are doing consistent actions every day, you will reach your goals.

May 12

"I believe my body wants to heal itself."

Your body is amazing, including having the ability to heal itself. Give it the right nutrients and conditions and it will give you all it has.

May 13

"I am fearless."

Facing your fears is more easily said than done. But when we avoid our fears, they actually grow and dominate us. The only way "out" is "through". Make some manageable steps to break through your fear and don't be afraid to get professional help from a therapist if fear is still holding you back.

May 14

"I focus on my desires and goals."

Make your goals and dreams the focus of your day so that their attraction towards you is magnetically strong. Once they become a part of your mindset, they will come to you with magnetic force.

May 15

"I am open to a shift in energy in my life."

Quite often when we are creating change in our lives, we need to undergo an energy shift. It will feel like everything and nothing changing at the same time. Basically, you will be getting a new outlook or perspective that will allow you to accomplish the goals you have set. When it happens, you will be in super power mode.

May 16

"I am aligned with my purpose."

Some people search their whole lives and never find their true purpose. Don't be one of them. Listen quietly to your inner voice and remember the times in your life when you were most fulfilled. Volunteering your time will also help you find out what truly matters to you.

May 17

"I am courageous and brave."

Just go for it! Easier said than done. Bravery is a skill, the more you face your fears, the braver you will become. Try something out of your comfort zone, go for a jog in the park, or sign up for a course and learn something new.

May 18

"I am proud of myself for sticking to my plan."

It takes a lot of determination and dedication to see your plan through to fruition. Written goals, a positive attitude and rewarding yourself will help. Congratulate yourself for your hard work!

May 19

"I am patient while change is evolving in my life."

As we work towards our goals, we can't always understand the way our circumstances are unfolding. Trust that it is working out perfectly for you, and every event that happens is happening to get you closer to your goals.

May 20

"My hard work is rewarded with money."

The only surefire way to sustainable wealth is providing a valuable service or product to others. Once you are doing work that you are passionate about, people will be lining up to give you their money.

May 21

"I am feeling vibrant and full of energy today."

Vibrance implies energy is flowing in and out of you. If you have not been feeling vibrant lately, try meditating, spending time in nature, getting more sleep and try to smile more.

May 22

"Day by day, I am achieving my goals."

The journey of a thousand miles starts with a single step is an ancient Chinese proverb, and still rings true today. All that is needed is consistent effort and you will arrive at your destination.

May 23

"I am imagining how I will feel when I achieve my goals."

Find a quiet place to envision how you will feel when you have enough money to do what you please. Enough money to take that trip, buy that car or give some to someone in need. Perhaps your goals are to feel free, imagine how you will feel on a road trip with no obligations to worry about.

May 24

"An abundant life is normal for me."

By telling yourself that abundance is normal, your mind will believe you and abundance will easily flow to you. Reconsider what you think abundance is, when we align with our purpose, abundance naturally flows.

May 25

"I am courageous."

The true test of a person's character is their reaction under fire. How will you react when challenges try to derail you. Will you stand strong and soldier on or run and hide?

May 26

"Today, I will look for a new project that I enjoy."

Is there a hobby that you've enjoyed in the past and has be shelved for a busy lifestyle? Or something new that you've always wanted to try? Take some time out of your day to work on something for no reason other than enjoyment.

May 27

"I am ready to benefit from all the hard times I have overcome in my life."

For every sorrow there is a joy. These emotions have an incredible way of balancing. Think of the hard things you have overcome, some of us have a longer list than others. It's time to benefit from the things we have learned and use them to our advantage or to help others in similar situations.

May 28

"I am my biggest fan."

Try not to criticize yourself or be hard on yourself, supporting yourself is crucial to your success. Be proud of your accomplishments and congratulate yourself when you have a small success.

May 29

"Money comes to me with ease."

Work on becoming a money magnet. Some suggestions are: counting your money, putting up pictures of money around your house and always giving money to those in need when you have extra.

May 30

"I possess everything I need to be successful."

Everything you need, you already have. Maybe you haven't awoken some parts of yourself that are ready to spring into action. Be patient and supportive with yourself, and be open to ideas that pop up in your mind. You never know where they will lead.

May 31

"I take time to nourish my body and give it everything it needs."

If you are always on the go and have a hard time accessing good food, buy a bag of apples or oranges and keep them in your car. Nature has created most fruits with their own wrappers so you can easily bring some along with you.

June 1

"I work on my plans everyday until I reach my goals."

Your plan is your path to your goal. It's the yellow brick road, the path to a miracle. Stick to it and make some progress every day.

June 2

"My desires are on fire and burning hot."

In order to reach your goals, you must make your desires burning hot. Put your vision board near your bed so you can see it before you go to sleep and first thing when you wake up. If you can't sleep, stare at it. Imagine how you will feel when you have everything you want.

June 3

"Today, I will do the next right thing."

It is easy to get overwhelmed by all that goes on in a day as well as manifesting your goals. Think of a car on a long journey at night, it is dark and you can only see a short distance ahead of you. You know you have a destination, but you need to focus on the steps in front of you right now or you will never arrive. What needs to be done today? Get it done and cross it off your to-do list.

June 4

"I am transforming my life."

Many things are changing in your life. Don't be surprised if some things in your life appear to malfunction or stop working. When your energy changes, it affects everything around you. Some things just don't stack up anymore, time to upgrade them with things that are useful to you now.

June 5

"I attract everything I need for my journey to my goals."

You will need plenty of help along the way. Be open to accepting it from helpful people, or spend some time shopping in a store or online, when you see something that is useful, get it!

June 6

"I am receiving great abundance."

The flood gates are either open or closed. Once they open, hang on for a ride! Abundance means having more than you need, remember to give back when abundance starts to flow.

June 7

"Today, I choose to try something new to improve my health."

Yoga, boxing, juice bar, or acupuncture? What could you try today? You can also improve your brain health by taking some time to destress or by doing a crossword puzzle.

June 8

"I am dedicated to quality in all I do, and I put in extra effort."

It is worth it to go the extra mile and put the last finishing touches of quality into your project. If you don't, you risk your reputation as well as having to replace or redo what you have already done.

June 9

"I feel powerful."

You have the ability to change your life as well as affect the lives of others by providing a valuable product or service. When you are aligned with your purpose, the results you put into the world will make a great impact.

June 10

"I keep my eye on the prize."

Make sure your vision board or list of goals is in a place where you can see them often. If they are on your bathroom mirror or in your kitchen make copies for your car or take a photo on your phone to easily access at any time. Keep your eye on your goals and take day by day steps to get there.

June 11

"I am worthy of the best in all areas of my life."

Is your car getting run down, is your computer too slow, does your smart phone have a cracked screen? Time for an upgrade. You would be surprised at how much of your energy is taken up looking at a cracked screen or wondering when your car will break down.

June 12

"I am patiently waiting for all my planets to align."

You are making changes in several areas of your life and so it takes time for it all to come together and create a new harmonic life for yourself. One day everything will come together and you will be pleasantly shocked.

June 13

"I am manifesting my goals into my life."

You may have days where not much seems to happen towards reaching your goals. Continue to manifest them with your affirmations, vision boards and lists. We can't always see the progress but it is happening.

June 14

"Today, I pursue my desires."

Take some time today to really think about and feel your goals. How would you feel driving that new car? How would you feel lying on a beach and not being concerned with the worries of day to day life? Feel the sun and wind on your face. Never give up on your desires.

June 15

"I am creating my future."

You are the creator of your reality, although you can only do so much to change your circumstances today, you can plant seeds that you will reap in the future. Get planting!

June 16

"I am attracting success."

Being successful means creating results. Results don't always come instantly, be patient, you are attracting the outcome that you desire.

June 17

"I am being my authentic self, I make choices based on what I want."

You might have people in your life that always want to throw in their two cents about what you should be doing. This can get confusing and distracting from what you really want. This is why lists and vision boards are so important, to make you focus on what you know YOU want.

June 18

"I intentionally follow my plan to reach my goals every day."

Remember the plan is the actions you are have laid out and must take to reach your goals. Action is a powerful force bringing your goals closer to you.

June 19

"I respect this season of my life."

The longest day of the year is approaching and summer is here. Which season of your life are you in? Rest, growth, reflection, sowing or reaping?

June 20

"My life is purposeful and important."

If you live in a big city or even a small one, it is easy to feel insignificant at times. Know that you are just as important as anyone else and it is your birthright as a human being to fulfill YOUR dreams.

June 21

"I give and receive love."

Giving and receiving are essential parts in the flow of energy. Although they are separate actions, they need to work together to create your abundant life. You may need to practice each independently to keep love circulating. If either giving or receiving is blocked, it will block your whole flow of love.

June 22

"I am patient with my body while it heals itself."

Most things either get better or get worse. Nothing really stays the same. Make steps to improve your health everyday for the better.

Give your body proper nourishment and exercise and, in most cases, it will do the rest.

June 23

"I believe in myself."

Being supportive of yourself is a huge part of reaching your goals. You need to know that you are your biggest supporter. Don't ever let yourself down. Unwaveringly believe in yourself!

June 24

"I am financially independent."

There is hardly a better feeling than having your own money to do what you choose with. Financial independence remains a dream for many. Get to work on your plan for creating extra wealth, and when money comes in, invest some, give some away and enjoy some as well.

June 25

"I motivate myself to follow my plan to reach my goals."

Usually we try to focus on positive things and our new future. If you are feeling this isn't really enough to motivate yourself, try the opposite. Think about living in poverty and poor health and all the pain and problems that will arise if you don't get to work and reach your goals. The time for action is now!

June 26

"I am passionate about my work."

What would you do if you had a million dollars? This question has been used by many to find out what they would do if they didn't need to think about rent or the mortgage. So what would you be doing? Your answer holds the key to achieving your goals. Try to identify your true passion projects that inspire you, then think about how you could share them with others.

June 27

"I am in control of my life."

When circumstances feel out of control, either globally or locally, you might really need to repeat this all day. Some other ideas to help you feel more in control are: help other people, make some art or a physical project and also to appreciate the events occurring and learn from them.

June 28

"Achieving my goals is easy, because I stick to my plan."

Once you have your plan firmly in place. Do not waver from it, you can make adjustments along the way, but do not quit. Your plan is the path to your dreams.

June 29

"My body feels stronger each and every day."

Your health is key to enjoying your success that you are working so hard for. Remember to take time daily to tend to the needs of your body. Even if you feel fine, exercise and nutrition should be priorities in your life.

June 30

"I am brave and I stand up for myself."

If you come across someone trying to push you down or put you back in your place, this affirmation is especially important for you. You don't even need to utter a word, what is the use in talking to someone like this? Your brave actions will determine your future freedom.

July 1

"I am achieving greatness."

However you measure greatness, you can make it your reality. Maybe you want 7 figures in your bank account or finding your soulmate is your goal. Every human being is capable of greatness, if you are committed to sticking to your plan.

July 2

"Money comes to me easily and effortlessly."

Let wealth know that it is welcome to reside with you. With this affirmation, you will become a magnet for wealth.

July 3

"Everything is possible."

If you can dream it, you can achieve it. In fact, the more you dream or think of your goal, the closer it will come to you. Once you have established some key goals and plans for reaching them, you can work on finding practical ways to achieve them.

July 4

"I make great choices."

In most countries, free choice is a human right. Don't ever let anyone try to shame you for a choice you have made. Even if your choice resulted in dismal failure. Learning from failure is a hugely important part of achieving success. Failure is very valuable.

July 5

"I am good at multitasking, I get a lot done."

Usually our goals and dreams involve some kind of leisure time. Lying by a pool or on a beach. In order to have time to rest we need to make the most of our work time. Try to accomplish many things at once, don't overwhelm yourself, but try to think about outsourcing or delegating out some tasks that others can easily and quickly do for you.

July 6

"I believe I have value to offer the world."

There is only one you. You were created with a set of unique skills and talents that only you possess. Think about times in your life where you have felt important, maybe volunteering somewhere or helping a neighbour. What makes you feel valued? Do more of that.

July 7

"I am grateful for my body."

The body is the temple of the soul. Whether it is big or small, tall or short, treat it with the utmost gratitude, it is your body that allows your mind to achieve your goals.

July 8

"I am compassionate with myself and others."

Be kind, understanding and patient with yourself and others. Nobody gets it right every time, in fact most successes are the result of many failures. This is how we learn to do it right.

July 9

"I am patient with myself and rest when I need to."

Balance is important to remember. Eating right, resting, de- stressing and relaxing must be balanced with working hard. Be sure to take time to recharge, there are many benefits including increasing your creativity and even improving your immune system.

July 10

"I am feeling exceptionally strong today."

If you are not feeling strong today, try a couple jumping jacks to invigorate you. Try going to bed early and waking up early to help give you more energy.

July 11

"I am proud of myself for all I have accomplished so far."

Applaud yourself! The beginning is the hardest part, you are already headed in the right direction towards your goals.

July 12

"I am resilient and nothing can stop me."

Resilience is the ability to spring back into shape quickly after a setback, or not bending at all. Whatever comes along, quickly learn from it and move on. Never stop pursuing your goals.

July 13

"I always have enough money."

This affirmation will give you comfort in knowing that whatever you need, you can find a way to afford it. Once money starts to role in, it doesn't stop.

July 14

"I am on my journey to success."

The journey may be long and have twists and turns along the way. It can be hard to know where you are on your journey but have faith you will arrive at your destination.

July 15

"All is well."

If you are a worrier like me, or an over thinker, this affirmation will put you at ease and quiet your mind.

July 16

"I am focused on my goals."

Removing distractions from your life is an essential part of focusing on your goals. You need to put your energy into achieving your dreams. Try to eliminate time wasting bad habits, cut out unimportant TV shows and use your energy towards working on your plan.

July 17

"My bravery gets me where I want to go."

Bravery is using your courage and mental strength to face fear or difficulty. Be strong, and persevere through unfavourable circumstances.

July 18

"My success depends on my efforts."

Consistent and persistent effort and action will move you along your path. If you are feeling like success is still elusive, maybe it's time to put in more effort. Rest when you need to and work harder when you can.

July 19

"I celebrate my independence and my ability to follow my dreams."

There are few greater feelings than being independent and able to do what you choose without having to run it by anymore. Be proud of yourself for having the courage to follow your dreams.

July 20

"Failure is my ally."

Any sports hall of famer will tell you that the only reason they did well so many times is because they also failed more times than anyone else. They just tried more times than their peers. Do more. Do not fear failure, in fact welcome it and learn from it. Failure is just important as success because we can learn from it and come back stronger and smarter.

July 21

"My actions today, guarantee my results in the future."

The way to a successful future is to stop talking and take action now! What can you do today that will help your plan to your goals?

July 22

"My success is infinite."

You really can have all the success. But only if you eliminate doubt. Doubt is the killer of success, make a decision to arm yourself with affirmations close at hand when doubt creeps in.

July 23

"I will show up today and everyday."

95% of success is just showing up. Being there and being ready to get to work or to be of service will guarantee success.

July 24

"I am systematically doing positive actions according to my plan to reach my goals."

Make a to-do list of things that you need to do next. Keep it on your wall until each thing is accomplished and you can cross them all off. If you have been working on your plan for awhile, it's a great time to do a check in and make a list of actions that you need to do now.

July 25

"I trust myself."

Removing any lingering self-doubt is an important step in trusting yourself. Some things you can do to increase trust in yourself are: right down the things that you like about yourself, trust your intuition and follow your desires.

July 26

"I only put healthy food in my body."

Fruits and vegetables are healthy, sugar and fat are not. It's pretty simple. Save the indulgences for a special occasion, try to make healthy choices on regular days.

July 27

"I am transforming my life."

Everyday your life is changing. You are working towards your goals and becoming a new person. Affirmations, vision boards and a supportive network of people will help you achieve your transformation.

July 28

"I am strong and brave."

If you ever feel doubt creeping in, this affirmation will stop it in it's tracks. I say this if I wake up in the early morning worrying about everything that needs to be done.

July 29

"I easily find all the resources that I need."

Trust that what you need will come to you at the right time. As soon as you start looking, you will find what you need.

July 30

"I believe there is enough money for everyone."

More money for you doesn't mean you are taking anything away from anyone else. Life is an all you can eat buffet, take what you need and others are free to do the same.

July 31

"New doors are opening for me."

You may have to knock on a few doors before some open for you. Create your opportunities by looking for them. If you are not finding any new doors, you might have to close some old doors before new ones start to open for you.

8

August 1

"I generously give money to those in need."

The old practice of tithing, or giving a percentage of your income to those in need, may not be practical today. I encourage you to find a cause, Covenant house for teens, an animal rescue, or St. Jude's hospital for sick kids. Something powerful happens when you share with those in need. You will be put in charge of more money to distribute at your discretion.

August 2

"I am enthusiastic about my life."

Enthusiasm is contagious. When you exude enthusiasm is spreads to those around you and magic can happen. Choose your team of helpful people carefully and help to energize them with your positive, enthusiastic attitude.

August 3

"I do what makes my heart happy."

When your heart is happy, you are the sun in your own solar system, people are drawn to you because of your authentic joy. Not only is a happy heart essential for your bliss, but doctors attribute some element of health to having a happy heart.

August 4

"I choose to focus on myself and my goals."

Free yourself from distractions, instead of engaging in meaningless time fillers, make some choices to do things that help your plan. Try some behind the scenes research or meeting up with like-minded colleagues.

August 5

"I believe my talents and skills will earn me the money I desire."

The way to sustainable riches is by trading a product or service for money. What can you offer people? Spend some time thinking about a skill you have, that you enjoy, that you can offer to others.

August 6

"I love and appreciate my body."

Exercising and eating right will help you fight off illness and stress. Take care of your most important asset. You will want to be healthy to enjoy the fruits of your labour in the years to come.

August 7

"I am creating financial freedom for myself."

I think everyone in the world desires to be financially free. The difference is you have a burning desire and a solid plan to get there.

You are also fortunate to have opportunities available to you to make this a reality. Do some extra work on your plan today.

August 8

"I am persistent and will not stop until I reach my goals."

Persistence pays off. Persistence is the vehicle to take you on your path to your goals. You can rest but don't you quit.

August 9

"Practicing gratitude, brings me joy."

The benefits from practicing gratitude are nearly endless. They include, happier emotions including joy, health benefits, a gateway to abundance, making others around you happier and an increase in our self-esteem.

August 10

"I will get it done."

If you are like me, I sometimes start to worry about a project that I've been putting off or that is coming up. I repeat this affirmation to help me finish it quickly. Cross it off your to- do list!

August 11

"I am living my own truth and I believe my dreams are important."

Others will have different dreams and likely don't share yours. Do what makes you happy. Try to distance yourself from unsupportive people and find a new team of like- minded people that are helpful and supportive on your journey to your goals.

August 12

"I do not accept anyones negative behaviour, it flows past me and leaves."

When change starts to happen in your life, don't be surprised if jealousy surges up from so called friends or even family members. See it for what it is, let it go through you and continue working on your plan to reach your goals.

August 13

"Luck is on my side."

Luck is considered to be favourable conditions that are brought merely by chance rather than by ones own efforts. It has been shown however, that one can create their own luck. The best way is by hard work, also by being positive and being on the lookout for luck.

August 14

"Today, I am the best version of myself."

We live many versions of ourselves over the years. It's time for the best You 5.0. Some ways to accomplish this are: by listing your favourite affirmations and reading them regularly, by eliminating anything unhealthy or toxic, and by appreciating failure and learning from it.

August 15

"I have a burning desire to achieve my goals."

Burning desire is what will guarantee your unwavering commitment to reaching your goals. You must make your desire so strong that quitting or failing is not an option. Envision how you will feel with your new house or pool, look at your vision board as much as possible.

August 16

"My skills are exceptional and I am financially rewarded for them."

Try to focus on quality, go the extra mile with your products or services. Your customers and clients will appreciate it and they are the bread and butter on your journey to riches.

August 17

"I am always attracting abundance."

Gratitude is the best way to attract abundance. Be grateful for all you have and continue looking at your vision board regularly to attract an even more abundant future. Giving your extra money away to people that need it is also a sure- fire way to increase the abundance headed your way.

August 18

"Amazing things are entering my life."

Small miracles are happening everyday, you just need to look for them. Miracles of life, love and nature are all around us. Appreciating the small amazements will bring bigger ones into your life.

August 19

"I invest in myself and in my future."

Find ways of planting more seeds today that you can reap in the future. Whether it is investing a small amount financially, buying some starter supplies for your business or taking a course in something you are interested in. Do it now, your future self will thank you!

August 20

"Success is magnetically attracted to me."

What is success? Success is the state of meeting your desired goals. It is the opposite of failure. The secret to success is planning, hard work and learning from failure. When failure comes up, embrace it and learn from it, we are ready for success now!

August 21

"My goals are BIG, and I can't wait to accomplish them."

Why make your goals BIG? Big goals get us excited, they force us to make a really good plan and they force us to do more and do it faster. Once you reach a goal, you will be thankful that you made it big.

August 22

"Today, I will practice gratitude for the achievements I have already made."

Gratitude will give your joy. Thank yourself and others that have helped you for what you have already done. Being gracious will allow additional, bigger achievements to become your reality.

August 23

"I attract people into my life that help me reach my goals."

You will need a helpful team of positive people to reach your goals. For every big accomplishment I've done in my life, I can count at least 10+ characters that have been essential in getting it done. The lawyer that does your paper work, the supplier you found online or the helper you hire. Choose your team wisely and treat them kindly.

August 24

"I receive unexpected money."

Check your bank account or go for a walk and look around. Consider buying someone a cup of coffee or helping someone else with extra money you find. I lost 50 dollars once, I hope the person that found it did something positive with it.

August 25

"I eat well and exercise regularly."

A healthy lifestyle will help your sleep and your mood. You need to be on top of your game for your journey to your goals. It might be long and you never know what challenges you will have to overcome, so be ready!

August 26

"I accept myself unconditionally."

In order to accept yourself unconditionally, you must know yourself through and through, even the darkest corners. Spending time alone will uncover you deepest feelings, once you have done this, then accept and never judge yourself. Be your own supporter and love all parts of yourself.

August 27

"Prosperity flows towards me."

Prosperity is very dynamic in nature, it comes from an exchange of your goods or services for what you want in return, usually money. In order to flourish and thrive you need to keep the dynamic going, give away your extra to keep prosperity flowing back to you.

August 28

"I comfort myself and give myself everything I need."

You are really stretching yourself on your journey to your goals. You are learning a lot and changing a lot in a short amount of time. Give yourself what you need to feel comforted and be patient with yourself as you travel to your dreams.

August 29

"I am in control of my life and my decisions."

You may need to become aware of healthy boundaries with others. Educate yourself if needed, so that you know where your healthy boundaries are. If you are finding that others are not respecting your life and decisions, then you are free to demand respect. It is your life, no one else's.

August 30

"I am becoming mentally stronger everyday."

Don't be defeated by fear, if you feel it creeping in, find your favourite affirmations and repeat them as often as possible. As you stumble towards success, you will become stronger everyday, remain positive and continue to challenge yourself to try and be open to new ideas. Slowly but surely, you will become mentally resilient.

August 31

"My confidence in myself continues to grow every day."

Self-confidence is a bonus you will get from your journey. As you continue to make good decisions and work hard, you will accept and trust yourself more each day.

September 1

"Today, I attract miracles into my life."

Miracles can happen, look around, they are happening every day. Flowers blooming in the spring, children being born, people healing illness. A positive, clean mind is a garden for miracles.

September 2

"I take time every day to improve my health."

Your body is your biggest asset, you need it to last a long time. Make time every day to eat healthily and exercise. Put a reminder or even two in your phone so that you can stop what you are doing and focus on your health, even for a short time each day.

September 3

"Having lots of money is normal for me."

By repeating this affirmation, your brain will think that it is normal for you to have lots of money and your reality will be forced to catchup.

September 4

"I believe in myself and my skills and talents."

You have to be the first one to believe in yourself before anyone else will. By believing in yourself, you build your self-confidence. Your skills and talents are unique, you just need to figure out how you can share them with others.

September 5

"I am creating prosperity in my life by taking action."

There is no time like the present to take action. Have a look at your action plan for your path to your goals, what can you do today to work on your plan?

September 6

"Success comes quickly and easily to me."

Stop trying so hard at things that aren't meant to be. Many success stories happen after someone has given up completely on forcing things that just suck their energy. Once you give up unrealistic plans, something happens, it clears the way for true success, built on things you enjoy and love to do.

September 7

"I always give my best effort and it is enough."

Give all you have when you are making a product or providing a service. Go above and beyond, customers will greatly appreciate this as most quality has slumped in recent years. Loyal customers are a big part of your team.

September 8

"I see abundance everywhere I look."

Some suggestions for seeing and feeling extra abundance are: start a savings account or even a "spare" coin or bill collection in a container, give back to others if you have extra money and try to enjoy the fine things you own. Use your nice dishes for no reason or put on your fancy clothes to go grocery shopping.

September 9

"I give my body the nourishment it needs to heal and maintain health."

Your body wants to be healthy. It is it's natural state. Giving it proper nutrients, cutting out sugar and fat and exercising regularly will give your body what it needs to heal and maintain itself.

September 10

"I believe in myself."

Believing in yourself can make or break your plans. Anything you can imagine, is something you can achieve. Believe you have the ability to do it. If you don't, who will? You must be your biggest supporter.

September 11

"New ideas and opportunities arrive just when I need them."

New opportunities don't come along every day, when they do, be sure to seize them. As you travel on your path to your goals keep your eyes open so you can recognize a great opportunity when one presents itself.

September 12

"I believe everything is unfolding as it is meant to be."

Having faith in a universal power will give you reassurance that everything is working perfectly. If things aren't moving as fast as you would like, be patient. Take whatever small steps you can take today to move you closer to your goals.

September 13

"I receive new sources of income."

Maybe an opportunity will come to you or maybe you need to create your own opportunity. There are many ways of generating new income streams: start a YouTube Channel, create a website that sells something or go door to door with a homemade craft or creation.

September 14

"I am following my heart."

Don't be afraid to follow your heart. Fear is the biggest roadblock, fear of what people will think or fear of what problems may lay ahead. Be brave, your heart will always lead you in the right direction if you are courageous enough to listen.

September 15

"I am full of energy today."

If you need an energy boost today, try taking a walk or drinking a healthy juice drink. Other things that suck up our energy are clutter and not having boundaries with pushy people.

September 16

"I am confident in my abilities."

Accepting yourself and realizing what you are capable of and what you are not, will help you really maximize your abilities. Once you know what you are good at, go for it! Make the most of what you are good at and what you enjoy.

September 17

"I balance my work, play and rest."

Balance is more important than ever these days. Family, work, and other commitments are relentless and demanding. Be your own scheduler, you may have to write down a schedule and stick to it. Make sure you can fit in everything that is important to you, including time for health and rest.

September 18

"I remain optimistic regardless of any challenges that arise."

Optimism is having faith in your successful outcome. When challenges arise, try to focus on the solution rather than the problem, don't dwell on it, fix it and move on.

September 19

"I am free of excuses."

Excuses are a barricade to success. Excuses will keep you stuck, they are like a flat tire on the road to your dreams and goals. They are useless, throw them in the garbage and get on with your plan.

September 20

"My potential is limitless."

There is no end to what you can achieve. You already have some goals you are working on, but after you accomplish those, you can set new, even bigger ones.

September 21

"I can solve any problem because I am smart."

Take responsibility for problems that arise, this means "responding-ably". You have the power to fix things, you know yourself well and can come up with a solution.

September 22

"The seeds I sow today, I will reap soon."

Sometimes it's hard to imagine the fruits of our labour. Continue to tend and care for the small seeds of success you are planting. Trust that the actions you are taking today, will pay off in the future, be patient.

September 23

"I am excited about the journey to my goals and welcome everything along my path."

Hopefully your plan consists of something you are enthusiastic about. It makes all the difference when challenges arise.

September 24

"Good things are happening to me."

Focusing on the good things throughout the day, will only bring more good. What we focus on expands and becomes more powerful. Take note and give gratitude for the small blessings that come up through the day.

September 25

"I have abundant vitality because I am aligned with my purpose."

Do what you love and you will always love what you do. Once you find your true passion, whether it is your full time job, a side gig or a hobby, you will be invigorated with a new energy. One that comes from deep inside and gives you joy.

September 26

"I am persistent and will never give up on my goals."

Quitting is not an option. If you are ever feeling unmotivated, it's time to step up your plans to reach your goals. I suggest making a new additional vision board with some fabulous photos of houses, cars, relationship photos or whatever it is that you desire. Lets get that drive back so we can get what we want!

September 27

"I am proud of my bravery."

Your behaviour and your character are what defines you as brave. Since you are making courageous steps to reach your goals, you should feel content with and grateful to yourself for getting you where you want to go, to your dreams!

September 28

"Being wealthy is normal for me."

This affirmation will make your mind think wealth is normal and already here. You will feel like you have already reached your financial goals. Once your mindset is programmed to that of a wealthy person, your reality and your bank account will quickly catch up.

September 29

"I trust my intuition."

Trust your gut, if someone or something feels off, then scrap it. It is a great feeling to walk away, or toward, what we determine is the best for ourselves. As you continue to make good decisions towards reaching your goals, your intuition will get sharper, and easier to uncover and understand. Try to listen to that quiet voice telling you what is best for yourself.

September 30

"I am enjoying NOW."

The present is called the present because it is a gift. Although we have big plans for the future, now is all we are guaranteed. Enjoy the moment, it is powerful. If you need to change something or do something important, don't wait. Do it now.

October 1

"I am taking care of my body."

Rest, exercise and diet are so important to your body. You only get one body, it will be with you your whole life. Sometimes we take better care of our car than our body. Time to realize what is important and make time, and a list, to keep us on track to form some healthy habits for our body's well being.

October 2

"My actions are courageous."

It takes courage and bravery to ditch the status quo and go in search of a way to reach our goals. Continue to take action, this is the only way to achieve success and reach your dreams.

October 3

"I make great choices."

I used to struggle between choice A and choice B. As I got older, it became easier. Why? I learned to trust my intuition, to listen to that tiny voice inside, and also to believe that even if my choice doesn't work out how I wished, I will learn from it and come back stronger.

October 4

"I am being helped"

When we bravely start on our path to our goals, something happens. It's as if the forces of the universe recognize your desire and help you along your way. Start and you will be helped.

October 5

"I attract the wealth I desire."

Some tips to help you become a money magnet are: count your money regularly, visualize yourself being wealthy and keep track of all the prosperity that comes to you and give much gratitude when it does.

October 6

"I feel strong and full of energy."

Some ways to help you feel strong and energetic are: take a walk, declutter, follow a powerful influencer on social media, clean up your house or listen to some invigorating music.

October 7

"I am safe."

Sometimes anxiety and worries about the future get the better of us. Time to comfort and calm yourself with this affirmation. How will you pay a certain bill? Not to worry, you will be safe no matter what and you will figure out a way to meet your obligations.

October 8

"I am attracting love into my life."

Be the embodiment of love. Spread it wherever you go. Love is a two way street, in order to receive it, you must give it. If you are looking for your soulmate, spend time envisioning them and how you will feel when you meet them.

October 9

"I conquer anxious feelings with action."

Action is the killer of anxiety. If you are feeling anxious, it is because something needs to be done and you are putting it off or not confronting it head on. Be brave. Deal with it so you can move on.

October 10

"I am open to limitless possibilities."

Once abundance starts to flow in your life, you never know what could happen. When you are aligned with your purpose and are doing things that are best for you, great things will just continue to grow and expand.

October 11

"I am creating powerful change."

When you make the decision to create change in your life, there is no turning back. It's a one way ticket to success. Your old life is not coming back, be excited for the new things coming to you slowly but surely.

October 12

"I fulfill my own needs and wants."

You will need a team of supportive people along your journey, but don't count on any of them to fulfill your needs or your wants. That is up to you. If you want a coffee or need a day off, arrange it for yourself, no need to explain anything to anyone.

October 13

"I attract helpful people into my life."

Some people genuinely want to see you succeed and some do not. When you find a selfless person that wants to help you succeed, they are like gold, treat them as such and be eternally grateful for their unconditional help and support.

October 14

"Every day that I am alive is a gift."

Although we have big plans for the future, the power of NOW is incredible. Enjoy today, call someone you love, you never know when it will be your last chance.

October 15

"I am the architect of my future."

Now that you are in charge of creating your future, and reaching your goals, get ready for change. Getting used to change is a funny thing because change is always changing. Get comfortable with change and embrace it. Your journey, is a journey, along the way everything changes.

October 16

"Brilliant ideas come easily to me."

Some people believe that brilliant ideas come to us by chance. Regardless of how we get them, we need to act on them in such a way as to make them useful to other people. If we can't make use of the brilliant idea, then it will either fade away or someone else will get the idea and use it.

October 17

"My dreams are becoming my reality."

Every day that you are working towards your goals, is one day closer to your dreams. Continue to work hard, don't make excuses and learn from challenges.

October 18

"I have faith in myself."

As you get to know your strengths, you can focus on what you are good at and make it part of your plans. If you have a talent, put it to work and earn some money towards your goals. Believe in your own abilities to be successful.

October 19

"My success is beginning now."

The intentional actions that you choose today will determine your results. Choose some actions that will get you results that help you reach your goals. Do them now.

October 20

"I attract positive and supportive people into my life."

Practice being the positive person you want to attract. Clear out any negativity, be honest with yourself and others and practice being supportive, this will attract supportive and positive people.

October 21

"Incredible opportunities are always coming to me."

When opportunity comes calling, be ready to greet it. Be on guard for great opportunities and when they present themselves, go for it! If you fail to recognize an opportunity someone else will seize it from you.

October 22

"I am patient and understanding with myself and others."

Being in control of our own emotions will help with patience when challenges arise. Sometimes deadlines are missed or things just don't go as planned. Endure the difficulty until a solution can be found, in short, make the best of it and learn what you can.

October 23

"I am motivated and focused."

If you are having a hard time staying motivated, break down your goal into some smaller steps and reward yourself regularly for the effort you put in.

October 24

"I am grateful for the money I receive."

Money loves attention. When you receive money, count it, look at it or enjoy the numbers in your banking app. This will help keep the flow of money coming towards you.

October 25

"I listen to my body and hear what it needs to be healthy."

Is there something you've been ignoring? Maybe you're overtired or have put on a few extra pounds from lack of exercise. Make a bigger effort to be healthy, make a list of daily goals and stick to it.

October 26

"I am financially free."

Imagine what it will feel like to not have any bills, mortgage or rent to pay. To be able to buy anything or travel anywhere you want. To have security for the rest of your life. The more you think about it, the closer it will come to your reality.

October 27

"Today, I feel joyful and I spread it to others."

Being thankful for the small things around you will help you feel joy today. Try thanking others for being good friends, it will help spread the feeling of joy.

October 28

"I make healthy choices to nourish my body."

If you have a few guilty pleasures, try replacing them with a healthier choice. There really are great products that are also healthy. Be open to trying something new.

October 29

"I choose to be happy."

Make the choice to focus on happiness, not on things that annoy you. Instead of cursing in traffic, try to think understanding, kind thoughts instead. Count your blessings and try to smile today.

October 30

"I am excited for the opportunities today brings."

You have many choices today: which way to walk to work, who you talk to, what you read or watch for entertainment.

With each choice, different opportunities will present themselves, enjoy the adventure of today.

October 31

"I am productive and positive."

Start being productive by solving your existing problems and stop wasting time. By solving problems, the door opens to positivity and leads the way to being really productive.

11

November 1

"I have all the energy I need to accomplish my goals."

It may seem like the path to your goals is a long one. Think of driving a car on a journey, you must focus on what is front of you now so that you reach your destination safely. Some tips for more energy are: drink more water, only drink coffee in the morning and exercise.

November 2

"I control my thoughts."

Control your thoughts or they will control you. Affirmations will help you control your thoughts and program your mind so you can get the results you desire.

November 3

"My life is an adventure and I plan the course."

Try to enjoy all the ups and downs that come with being alive. You can chart the course by setting some big goals, but the events on your path are yet to be determined.

November 4

"I radiate success."

Fake it until you make it. Imagine you have already succeeded, how will you feel? What will you wear? Will you spend time worrying about little unimportant things, or get on with bigger things that further contribute to your success?

November 5

"Change is easy and gets me closer to my goals."

Change is not always easy but to reach your goals there will be constant change. So if you can make yourself believe that change is easy and enjoy change, you will have an easier time achieving your dreams.

November 6

"I am attracting supportive people into my life."

Try to be the person you want to attract. Try being supportive to those around you, not judging and only offering positive comments.

November 7

"Money flows to me from all directions."

Multiple streams of income are a great idea if one of your goals is to have more money. Try selling something that you have made: wood working or plants from your garden are some ideas.

November 8

"I create new healthy habits to replace old outdated ones."

Your journey is dynamic, you might be surprised when you realize some of your old habits are not needed anymore. Watching TV before bed can be replaced with watching an educational video or reading something that will help you achieve your goals faster.

November 9

"I am grateful for all my experiences and achievements."

Gratitude will bring you more positive opportunities. Praise yourself for what you have accomplished so far. All the events that have happened in your life have made you the person you are today. Be grateful for all of them.

November 10

"The extra money I receive helps others."

Be sure to give away some of your money to help others. When you do this, it triggers something. The universe will give you more money to divide up how you see fit. Try to find a cause or a charity that is important to you.

November 11

"I believe in myself."

Know that you can overcome anything. You must support yourself 100% in order to get yourself to your goals. They are your goals and you are the only one that can get yourself there.

November 12

"I will persevere until I reach my goals."

It is the struggle and the hard times that will really make you appreciate success once you arrive. Keep on, keeping on, it will be worth it one day.

November 13

"I am confident in myself and believe in my abilities."

Every challenge along the way will make you stronger and increase your self-confidence. Don't focus on mistakes of the past, learn from them and use them to propel yourself forwards.

November 14

"I am unstoppable."

Think of yourself as a bulldozer, slow, strong and unstoppable. Slowly pushing everything unneeded aside and making a nice path towards your dreams.

November 15

"I am open to new solutions."

Is there a challenge that keeps reoccurring? It's time for some good old-fashioned brainstorming. Take a pen and paper and write the challenge in the middle with a circle around it, draw branches coming off it with more circles with some possible solutions inside them. You never know what you will come up with.

November 16

"Magic is all around me."

If you can't feel everyday magic today, try gardening in the dirt, doing some hands on finger painting or watching the sun rise or set. Magic is found in childish, simple pleasures.

November 17

"I read my goals everyday so that they become who I am now."

The more you look at your vision board, read and write out your goals and practice your daily affirmations, the more you are reprogramming your mind. You are actually becoming these things that once were only a dream.

November 18

"I am happy with myself, and I am the only one that matters."

What others think of you is not your concern. A LOT of energy is wasted on people caring about what others think.

November 19

"I am creating incredible wealth."

Spend some time investigating the three main types of income some more. They are earned, portfolio and passive income. Which one do you need to expand?

November 20

"I feel fit and strong."

You will need energy to complete your journey to your goals. Drink more water, exercise daily and make healthy dietary choices. Write down a daily list of goals if you need to.

November 21

"My bravery gets me through anything."

Be confident that you will stand tall and fight when you need to. Your courage will get through what ever comes your way.

November 22

"I am attracting new opportunities into my life."

Look in the areas of your passions for new opportunities. Try volunteering or learning more about one of your favourite topics to create some new opportunities of your own.

November 23

"I will keep trying and never give up until I reach my goals."

If at first you don't succeed, try again! You will come back stronger and wiser. Use failure as a stepping stone to success, if you are feeling defeated, take a rest to regroup and then get back at it!

November 24

"I am aligned with my purpose."

When you are aware of your passions and what you are truly excited about and meant to do in your life, things will fall into place. Not only will you thoroughly enjoy your days but there are also numerous ways to make your passion into a way to earn income.

November 25

"I create my circumstances with the intentional actions I take."

Focus on your ideas and thoughts of your goals, and remember the plan you have to get there. Take action today that will help move you along your path.

November 26

"I trade my hard work for an abundance of money."

True wealth can only come from selling a product or providing a service. Every second of your day is valuable, find a way to get monetarily rewarded for trading your valuable time.

November 27

"Everything is working out perfectly for me."

We can't always see the big picture, nor do we know how all the pieces will fit together. Trust that now that you are aligned with your dreams and goals, everything is working itself out to benefit you.

November 28

"I release all that doesn't serve me, to make room for what I desire now."

Sometimes we have to make room for what is coming. If you feel unproductive or blocked, it's time for some housecleaning. Either mentally release what isn't working for you anymore or physically give some old furniture to the goodwill and make room for what you want now.

November 29

"I am my biggest supporter."

Be the parent to yourself that you always wished you had. Tell yourself: "you can do it" and "I believe in you'.

November 30

"Attaining my goals is so close I can feel them."

Once you start working on your plan to your goals, you are effectively becoming part of your success. You may not be there yet, but you are getting close!

12

December 1

"I am achieving whatever I set my mind to."

Remember, your brain is the original computer, if you give it the right input, the output is almost certainly guaranteed. Be careful what you put into your brain today, it will take your directions and act on them.

December 2

"My dreams are becoming my reality."

When you reach your goals, what will you do differently? Go to a fancy restaurant or buy some nice clothes? Treat yourself now, it will make reaching your dreams that much easier and natural.

December 3

"I am productive."

Some people find multi-tasking productive, while others get overwhelmed by it. Do what works for you, you may need to make a daily to-do list and just do one thing at time and then enjoy crossing it off.

December 4

"My confidence gets me through tough days."

Be confident in yourself and believe that you will be there to pick yourself up and dust yourself off when needed. There will always be tough days, try to take care of yourself so you can recover quickly and get back at it.

December 5

"I enjoy meeting other people and make new friends easily."

Even though you are responsible for achieving your goals, there will be many characters that help you along the way. Be open to networking and meeting new supportive people with a similar mindset.

December 6

"I am comfortable in my own skin."

Stop caring about what others think. You know yourself the best and you know what you are capable of. Working on personal issues and weaknesses privately will help you feel more confident with yourself.

December 7

"I am my own hero."

Stop waiting for the perfect person to enter your life, fix everything and rescue you. You are your own hero, be the person that fixes everything and rescue yourself.

December 8

"I motivate myself."

Are you self-motivated? If your answer is no, is time to dig deep and find a passion project. Think back to the best times in your life, what were you doing? When you are engaging in a meaningful project or venture, motivation will be inherent.

December 9

"My actions take me closer to my greater purpose."

You can only do so much in a day, choose wisely and focus on actions that will get you where you want to go.

December 10

"I am financially free."

Try to save a bit of your income and pay off your debts. Give away some of your hard earned money and always look for opportunities to create more income.

December 11

"I am proud of myself and what I have already accomplished."

Be proud of how far you have come and how hard you are trying. Be proud of your goal setting and efforts thus far. It takes a lot of courage to follow your dreams.

December 12

"I take care of myself and rest when I need to."

Listen to your body, when it's time to rest be sure that you do. Your body will thank you and be rejuvenated.

December 13

"I can barely contain my excitement for the future."

Take another look at your vision board, imagine how you will feel when you achieve your goals. How will you feel driving your new car or moving into your new house?

December 14

"I am ambitious."

Ambition means always striving to reach your goals. Never stopping. Hard work, perseverance and dedication will get you there.

December 15

"I am ready to receive abundance in all areas of my life."

Giving gratitude for the small things and clearing the way to welcome new opportunities in all areas, will invite abundance into your life.

December 16

"Every challenge that happens gets me one step closer to my goals."

Think of the path to your goals as riddled with challenges. If we can learn from the challenge we can move past it and continue on. Again, if we bypass the lesson and try to take a short cut, unlearned challenges will always show up again.

December 17

"Today I will give my body what it needs."

Do you need more sleep? Take a nap today. Do you need some exercise? Go for a walk. Do you need to just sit and do nothing? Whatever comes to your mind, do that.

December 18

"My new energy is strong!"

At times when I've had a big energy shift in my own life, many things and people around me have acted strangely. My computer broke down because I was inspired and used it so much, my tooth chipped because I was exuberant with energy. People in your life may not respond positively, be kind and carry on.

December 19

"Money comes to me easily."

Make your self a money magnet. Remember sustainable wealth can only come from providing a valuable product or service to others. Practice gratitude for the money you receive in exchange for your product or service. Visualize money coming to you easily.

December 20

"I appreciate everything I have in my life."

Focus on the good in your life and appreciate it. Don't dwell on the negatives that pop up. Just fix them, appreciate what you have learned and move on. Appreciating everything will open the door to what you desire.

December 21

"My inner light is growing brighter."

It is always darkest before the dawn. It is the darker times that make us appreciate when light returns. Enjoy the Winter Solstice, for tomorrow longer days will return.

December 22

"I feel calm, confident, and powerful."

There is no need to worry, everything is working as it should, be patient, your goals are getting closer and closer to you every day. Enjoy where you are and be proud of your accomplishments.

December 23

"Everything in my life is a blessing."

Things that you might think are just a nuisance, are actually blessings. You can learn just as much from bothersome things, as from favourable events.

December 24

"I am able to concentrate on my work so I can reach my goals."

Eliminating distractions will help with concentrating your energy. Some other tips for improving concentration are: take an exercise break, play some brain concentration games or turn off music or noise while you are working.

December 25

"I practice giving and receiving."

Giving and receiving are two sides of the same coin. It is important to practice both separately so that they can flow together and keep you in tune with universal abundance.

December 26

"I inspire others."

Be the inspiring person you wish you knew. Don't micromanage others, help them to find purpose in what they do as well. By helping and inspiring others we can transform our lives as well as the lives of others.

December 27

"I continue to follow my plan and get closer to my goals everyday."

We don't know exactly how long our journey is to reach our desired goals. As long as you stay on your path and follow your plan, you will get there, one step at a time.

December 28

"Miracles are happening in my life."

Clearing out space in your mind and your life will open the door to miracles. If you want to see a miracle, watch the sun rising and setting or plant some seeds and watch what happens.

December 29

"I am achieving my financial goals, and I will not stop until I do."

Persistence and confidence will get you there. Know that you have all that is needed to reach your goals. Try putting up some more pictures of money around your house.

December 30

"I easily attract all that I desire."

Focus on your vision board, make it bigger if you need to. Continue to make time for focussing on your desires and keep manifesting them until they arrive.

December 31

"Everything I start, I finish strong."

When things get tough, will you settle for where you are, or will you push through and finish strong? The last few seconds of a race determine the winner and quite often the most points in sports games are scored in the final minutes. Keep going, the finish line is near!

Congratulations! You have finished an incredible year. Hopefully you are feeling empowered and closer to your goals. I would now encourage you to update your goals. Maybe you have achieved some small goals and your bigger goals are still in progress. Make a New Year's commitment to start another updated vision board and read this book again with your current goals in mind. All the best for the New Year!

One Year of
Gratitude Journaling

A 52 week daily guide to cultivating a grateful,
positive attitude and attracting abundance.

Nicole Lockhart

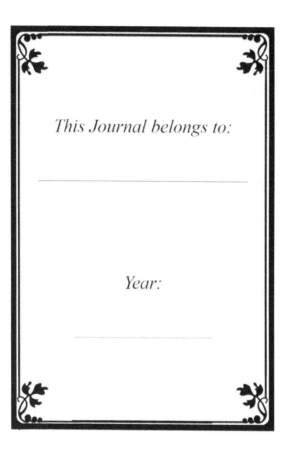

This Journal belongs to:

_____

Year:

_____

GRATITUDE

Cultivating an attitude of gratitude has been proven for thousands of years to bring inner joy, peace and prosperity to one's life. It also brings joy and peace to those around you. "Gratitude" has a Latin origin meaning "thankful" and "pleasing". It is one of life's great secrets that many people are rediscovering today.

grat•i•tude

\ ˈgra-tə-ˌtüd , -ˌtyüd \

: the quality of being thankful; readiness to show appreciation for and to return kindness.

It is no coincidence that gratitude and grace start with the same three letters, both come from the same word origin. When we adopt an attitude of gratitude, we are living in grace.

grace

\ ˈgrās \

: unmerited divine assistance given to humans for their regeneration or sanctification

: a state of sanctification enjoyed through divine assistance

When you are living life this way, everything will just seem to work out for you. Trust that the Universe will put you where you belong and help you along your life's journey to reach your goals and dreams.

So let's get started living your best possible life!

Week 1

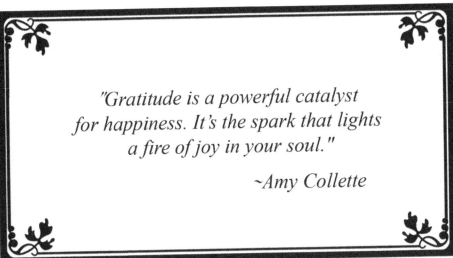

"Gratitude is a powerful catalyst for happiness. It's the spark that lights a fire of joy in your soul."

~Amy Collette

Today, I am grateful for:　　　　Date:_____

1)_____

2)_____

3)_____

Today, I am grateful for:　　　　Date:_____

1)_____

2)_____

3)_____

Today, I am grateful for:　　　　Date:_____

1)_____

2)_____

3)_____

Today, I am grateful for: Date:

1)_____

2)_____

3)_____

Today, I am grateful for: Date:

1)_____

2)_____

3)_____

Today, I am grateful for: Date:

1)_____

2)_____

3)_____

Today, I am grateful for: Date:

1)_____

2)_____

3)_____

This week:

Who made me smile?_____

Who inspired me?_____

What is the best thing that happened?_____

_____

What do I want to attract more of?_____

_____

Week 2

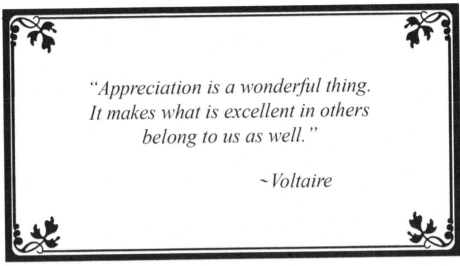

*"Appreciation is a wonderful thing.
It makes what is excellent in others
belong to us as well."*

~Voltaire

Today, I am grateful for: Date: _____

1)_____

2)_____

3)_____

Today, I am grateful for: Date: _____

1)_____

2)_____

3)_____

Today, I am grateful for: Date: _____

1)_____

2)_____

3)_____

Today, I am grateful for: Date:

1)_____

2)_____

3)_____

Today, I am grateful for: Date:

1)_____

2)_____

3)_____

Today, I am grateful for: Date:

1)_____

2)_____

3)_____

Today, I am grateful for: Date:

1)_____

2)_____

3)_____

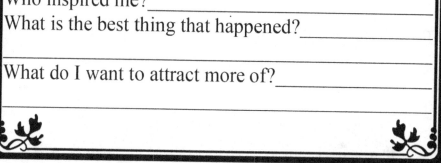

This week:

Who made me smile?_____

Who inspired me?_____

What is the best thing that happened?_____

_____

What do I want to attract more of?_____

_____

Week 3

"When we focus on our gratitude,
the tide of disappointment goes out
and the tide of love rushes in."

~Kristin Armstrong

Today, I am grateful for: Date:
1)
2)
3)

Today, I am grateful for: Date:
1)
2)
3)

Today, I am grateful for: Date:
1)
2)
3)

Today, I am grateful for: _____ Date: _____
1)_____
2)_____
3)_____

Today, I am grateful for: _____ Date: _____
1)_____
2)_____
3)_____

Today, I am grateful for: _____ Date: _____
1)_____
2)_____
3)_____

Today, I am grateful for: _____ Date: _____
1)_____
2)_____
3)_____

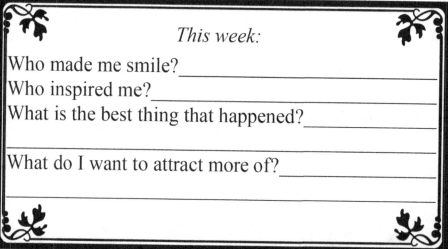

This week:

Who made me smile?_____

Who inspired me?_____

What is the best thing that happened?_____
_____

What do I want to attract more of?_____
_____

Week 4

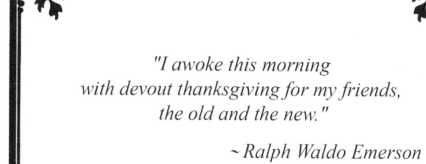

*"I awoke this morning
with devout thanksgiving for my friends,
the old and the new."*

~ Ralph Waldo Emerson

Today, I am grateful for: Date: _____

1) _____

2) _____

3) _____

Today, I am grateful for: Date: _____

1) _____

2) _____

3) _____

Today, I am grateful for: Date: _____

1) _____

2) _____

3) _____

Today, I am grateful for: _____ Date: _____

1)_____
2)_____
3)_____

Today, I am grateful for: _____ Date: _____

1)_____
2)_____
3)_____

Today, I am grateful for: _____ Date: _____

1)_____
2)_____
3)_____

Today, I am grateful for: _____ Date: _____

1)_____
2)_____
3)_____

This week:

Who made me smile?_____
Who inspired me?_____
What is the best thing that happened?_____
_____
What do I want to attract more of?_____
_____

Week 5

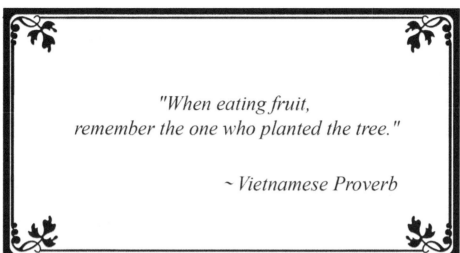

*"When eating fruit,
remember the one who planted the tree."*

~ Vietnamese Proverb

Today, I am grateful for: Date:_____
1)_____
2)_____
3)_____

Today, I am grateful for: Date:_____
1)_____
2)_____
3)_____

Today, I am grateful for: Date:_____
1)_____
2)_____
3)_____

Today, I am grateful for: Date: _____

1)_____

2)_____

3)_____

Today, I am grateful for: Date: _____

1)_____

2)_____

3)_____

Today, I am grateful for: Date: _____

1)_____

2)_____

3)_____

Today, I am grateful for: Date: _____

1)_____

2)_____

3)_____

This week:

Who made me smile?_____

Who inspired me?_____

What is the best thing that happened?_____
_____

What do I want to attract more of?_____
_____

Week 6

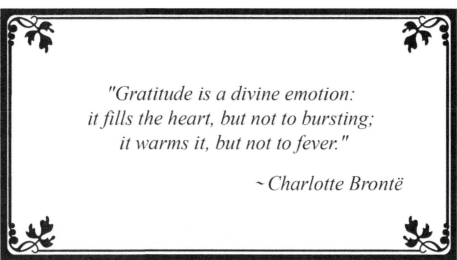

*"Gratitude is a divine emotion:
it fills the heart, but not to bursting;
it warms it, but not to fever."*

~ Charlotte Brontë

Today, I am grateful for:　　　Date:
1)_____
2)_____
3)_____

Today, I am grateful for:　　　Date:
1)_____
2)_____
3)_____

Today, I am grateful for:　　　Date:
1)_____
2)_____
3)_____

Today, I am grateful for: _____ Date: _____
1)_____
2)_____
3)_____

Today, I am grateful for: _____ Date: _____
1)_____
2)_____
3)_____

Today, I am grateful for: _____ Date: _____
1)_____
2)_____
3)_____

Today, I am grateful for: _____ Date: _____
1)_____
2)_____
3)_____

This week:

Who made me smile?_____
Who inspired me?_____
What is the best thing that happened?_____
_____
What do I want to attract more of?_____
_____

Week 7

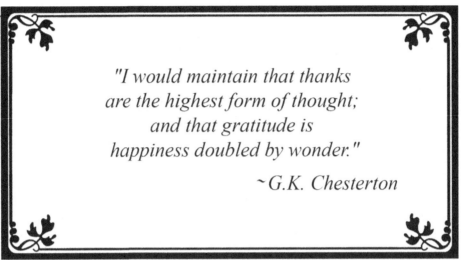

*"I would maintain that thanks
are the highest form of thought;
and that gratitude is
happiness doubled by wonder."*

~G.K. Chesterton

Today, I am grateful for: Date: _____

1)_____

2)_____

3)_____

Today, I am grateful for: Date: _____

1)_____

2)_____

3)_____

Today, I am grateful for: Date: _____

1)_____

2)_____

3)_____

Today, I am grateful for: _____ Date: _____
1)_____
2)_____
3)_____

Today, I am grateful for: _____ Date: _____
1)_____
2)_____
3)_____

Today, I am grateful for: _____ Date: _____
1)_____
2)_____
3)_____

Today, I am grateful for: _____ Date: _____
1)_____
2)_____
3)_____

This week:

Who made me smile?_____
Who inspired me?_____
What is the best thing that happened?_____
_____
What do I want to attract more of?_____
_____

Week 8

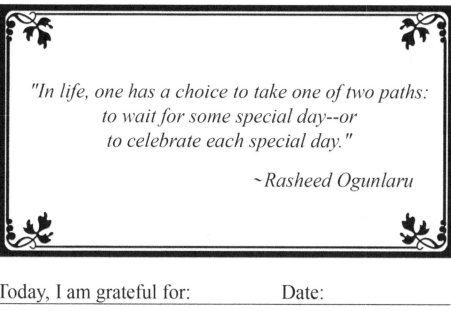

*"In life, one has a choice to take one of two paths:
to wait for some special day--or
to celebrate each special day."*

~Rasheed Ogunlaru

Today, I am grateful for: Date:
1)
2)
3)

Today, I am grateful for: Date:
1)
2)
3)

Today, I am grateful for: Date:
1)
2)
3)

Today, I am grateful for: Date:
1)_____
2)_____
3)_____

Today, I am grateful for: Date:
1)_____
2)_____
3)_____

Today, I am grateful for: Date:
1)_____
2)_____
3)_____

Today, I am grateful for: Date:
1)_____
2)_____
3)_____

This week:

Who made me smile?_____
Who inspired me?_____
What is the best thing that happened?_____
_____
What do I want to attract more of?_____
_____

Week 9

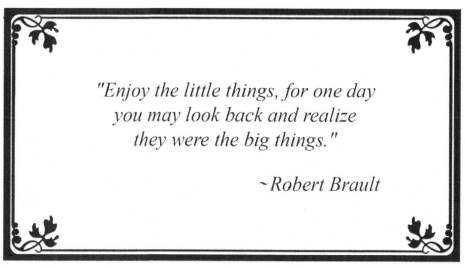

"Enjoy the little things, for one day you may look back and realize they were the big things."

~Robert Brault

Today, I am grateful for: Date:
1)_____
2)_____
3)_____

Today, I am grateful for: Date:
1)_____
2)_____
3)_____

Today, I am grateful for: Date:
1)_____
2)_____
3)_____

Today, I am grateful for: _____ Date: _____
1)_____
2)_____
3)_____

Today, I am grateful for: _____ Date: _____
1)_____
2)_____
3)_____

Today, I am grateful for: _____ Date: _____
1)_____
2)_____
3)_____

Today, I am grateful for: _____ Date: _____
1)_____
2)_____
3)_____

This week:

Who made me smile?_____
Who inspired me?_____
What is the best thing that happened?_____
_____
What do I want to attract more of?_____
_____

*"It's a funny thing about life,
once you begin to take note of the things
you are grateful for,
you begin to lose sight of the things that you lack."*
~ Germany Kent

Today, I am grateful for: Date:
1)_____
2)_____
3)_____

Today, I am grateful for: Date:
1)_____
2)_____
3)_____

Today, I am grateful for: Date:
1)_____
2)_____
3)_____

Today, I am grateful for: Date:
1)_____
2)_____
3)_____

Today, I am grateful for: Date:
1)_____
2)_____
3)_____

Today, I am grateful for: Date:
1)_____
2)_____
3)_____

Today, I am grateful for: Date:
1)_____
2)_____
3)_____

This week:

Who made me smile?_____
Who inspired me?_____
What is the best thing that happened?_____
_____
What do I want to attract more of?_____
_____

Week 11

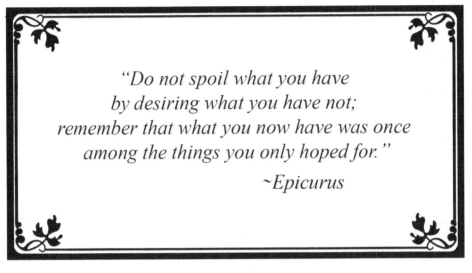

*"Do not spoil what you have
by desiring what you have not;
remember that what you now have was once
among the things you only hoped for."*

~Epicurus

Today, I am grateful for: Date:
1)
2)
3)

Today, I am grateful for: Date:
1)
2)
3)

Today, I am grateful for: Date:
1)
2)
3)

Today, I am grateful for: Date:

1)_____

2)_____

3)_____

Today, I am grateful for: Date:

1)_____

2)_____

3)_____

Today, I am grateful for: Date:

1)_____

2)_____

3)_____

Today, I am grateful for: Date:

1)_____

2)_____

3)_____

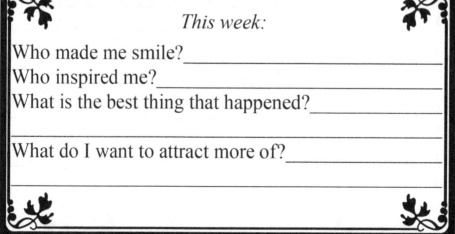

This week:

Who made me smile?_____

Who inspired me?_____

What is the best thing that happened?_____

_____

What do I want to attract more of?_____

_____

Week 12

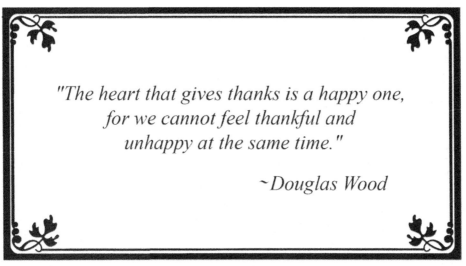

"The heart that gives thanks is a happy one, for we cannot feel thankful and unhappy at the same time."

~Douglas Wood

Today, I am grateful for: Date: _____
1)_____
2)_____
3)_____

Today, I am grateful for: Date: _____
1)_____
2)_____
3)_____

Today, I am grateful for: Date: _____
1)_____
2)_____
3)_____

Today, I am grateful for: Date: _____

1)_____

2)_____

3)_____

Today, I am grateful for: Date: _____

1)_____

2)_____

3)_____

Today, I am grateful for: Date: _____

1)_____

2)_____

3)_____

Today, I am grateful for: Date: _____

1)_____

2)_____

3)_____

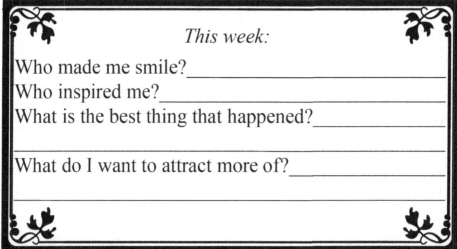

This week:

Who made me smile?_____

Who inspired me?_____

What is the best thing that happened?_____

_____

What do I want to attract more of?_____

_____

Week 13

*"Piglet noticed that even though he had a
Very Small Heart,
it could hold a rather large amount of Gratitude."*

~A.A. Milne, 'Winnie-the-Pooh'

Today, I am grateful for: Date: _____

1)_____

2)_____

3)_____

Today, I am grateful for: Date: _____

1)_____

2)_____

3)_____

Today, I am grateful for: Date: _____

1)_____

2)_____

3)_____

Today, I am grateful for: Date:

1)_____

2)_____

3)_____

Today, I am grateful for: Date:

1)_____

2)_____

3)_____

Today, I am grateful for: Date:

1)_____

2)_____

3)_____

Today, I am grateful for: Date:

1)_____

2)_____

3)_____

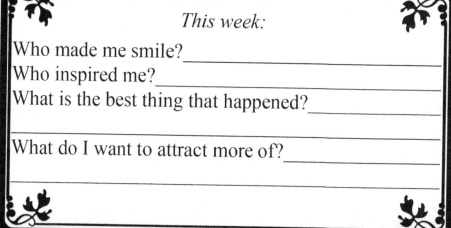

This week:

Who made me smile?_____

Who inspired me?_____

What is the best thing that happened?_____

_____

What do I want to attract more of?_____

_____

Week 14

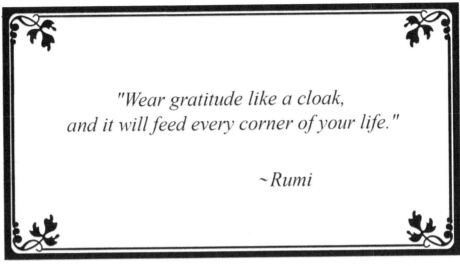

*"Wear gratitude like a cloak,
and it will feed every corner of your life."*

~ Rumi

Today, I am grateful for: Date:
1)
2)
3)

Today, I am grateful for: Date:
1)
2)
3)

Today, I am grateful for: Date:
1)
2)
3)

Today, I am grateful for: Date:_____
1)_____
2)_____
3)_____

Today, I am grateful for: Date:_____
1)_____
2)_____
3)_____

Today, I am grateful for: Date:_____
1)_____
2)_____
3)_____

Today, I am grateful for: Date:_____
1)_____
2)_____
3)_____

This week:

Who made me smile?_____
Who inspired me?_____
What is the best thing that happened?_____
_____
What do I want to attract more of?_____
_____

Week 15

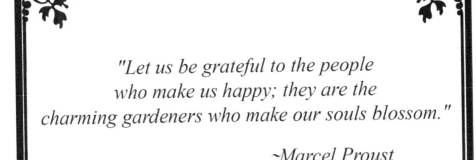

*"Let us be grateful to the people
who make us happy; they are the
charming gardeners who make our souls blossom."*

~Marcel Proust

Today, I am grateful for: Date: _____

1)_____

2)_____

3)_____

Today, I am grateful for: Date: _____

1)_____

2)_____

3)_____

Today, I am grateful for: Date: _____

1)_____

2)_____

3)_____

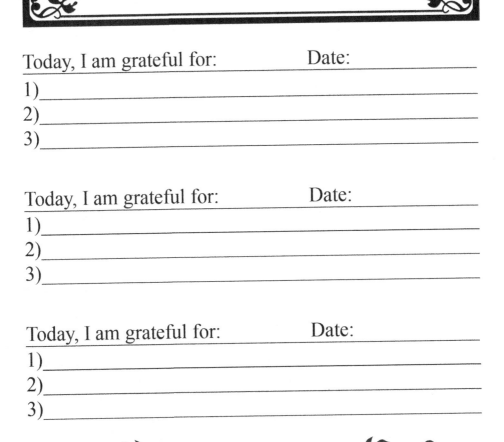

Today, I am grateful for: _____ Date: _____
1)_____
2)_____
3)_____

Today, I am grateful for: _____ Date: _____
1)_____
2)_____
3)_____

Today, I am grateful for: _____ Date: _____
1)_____
2)_____
3)_____

Today, I am grateful for: _____ Date: _____
1)_____
2)_____
3)_____

This week:

Who made me smile?_____
Who inspired me?_____
What is the best thing that happened?_____
_____
What do I want to attract more of?_____
_____

Week 16

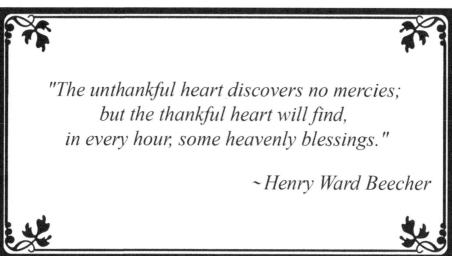

*"The unthankful heart discovers no mercies;
but the thankful heart will find,
in every hour, some heavenly blessings."*

~Henry Ward Beecher

Today, I am grateful for: Date:
1)_____
2)_____
3)_____

Today, I am grateful for: Date:
1)_____
2)_____
3)_____

Today, I am grateful for: Date:
1)_____
2)_____
3)_____

Today, I am grateful for: Date:

1)_____

2)_____

3)_____

Today, I am grateful for: Date:

1)_____

2)_____

3)_____

Today, I am grateful for: Date:

1)_____

2)_____

3)_____

Today, I am grateful for: Date:

1)_____

2)_____

3)_____

This week:

Who made me smile?_____

Who inspired me?_____

What is the best thing that happened?_____

_____

What do I want to attract more of?_____

_____

Week 17

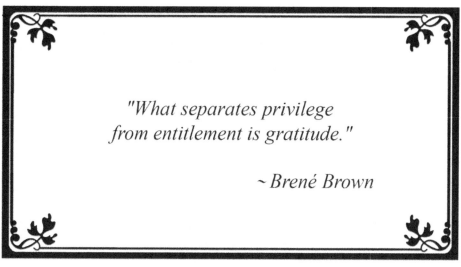

*"What separates privilege
from entitlement is gratitude."*

~ Brené Brown

Today, I am grateful for: Date:
1)_____
2)_____
3)_____

Today, I am grateful for: Date:
1)_____
2)_____
3)_____

Today, I am grateful for: Date:
1)_____
2)_____
3)_____

Today, I am grateful for: _____ Date: _____
1)_____
2)_____
3)_____

Today, I am grateful for: _____ Date: _____
1)_____
2)_____
3)_____

Today, I am grateful for: _____ Date: _____
1)_____
2)_____
3)_____

Today, I am grateful for: _____ Date: _____
1)_____
2)_____
3)_____

This week:

Who made me smile?_____
Who inspired me?_____
What is the best thing that happened?_____
_____
What do I want to attract more of?_____
_____

Week 18

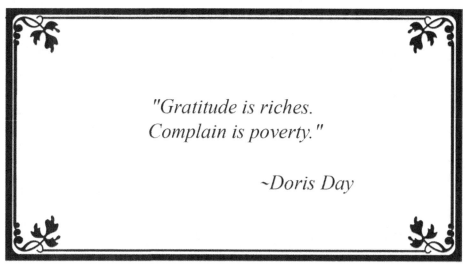

"Gratitude is riches.
Complain is poverty."

~Doris Day

Today, I am grateful for: Date: _____
1)_____
2)_____
3)_____

Today, I am grateful for: Date: _____
1)_____
2)_____
3)_____

Today, I am grateful for: Date: _____
1)_____
2)_____
3)_____

Today, I am grateful for: _____ Date: _____
1)_____
2)_____
3)_____

Today, I am grateful for: _____ Date: _____
1)_____
2)_____
3)_____

Today, I am grateful for: _____ Date: _____
1)_____
2)_____
3)_____

Today, I am grateful for: _____ Date: _____
1)_____
2)_____
3)_____

This week:

Who made me smile?_____
Who inspired me?_____
What is the best thing that happened?_____
_____
What do I want to attract more of?_____
_____

Week 19

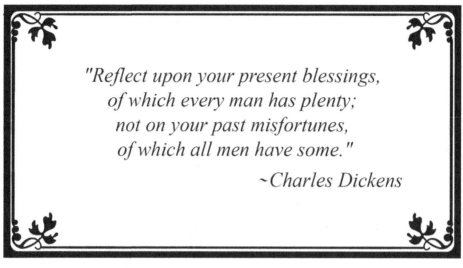

"Reflect upon your present blessings,
of which every man has plenty;
not on your past misfortunes,
of which all men have some."

~Charles Dickens

Today, I am grateful for: Date:
1)_____
2)_____
3)_____

Today, I am grateful for: Date:
1)_____
2)_____
3)_____

Today, I am grateful for: Date:
1)_____
2)_____
3)_____

Today, I am grateful for: _____ Date: _____

1)_____
2)_____
3)_____

Today, I am grateful for: _____ Date: _____

1)_____
2)_____
3)_____

Today, I am grateful for: _____ Date: _____

1)_____
2)_____
3)_____

Today, I am grateful for: _____ Date: _____

1)_____
2)_____
3)_____

This week:

Who made me smile?_____
Who inspired me?_____
What is the best thing that happened?_____
_____
What do I want to attract more of?_____
_____

Week 20

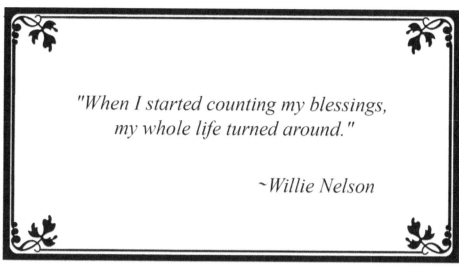

*"When I started counting my blessings,
my whole life turned around."*

~Willie Nelson

Today, I am grateful for: Date:

1)_____

2)_____

3)_____

Today, I am grateful for: Date:

1)_____

2)_____

3)_____

Today, I am grateful for: Date:

1)_____

2)_____

3)_____

Today, I am grateful for: Date:

1)_____

2)_____

3)_____

Today, I am grateful for: Date:

1)_____

2)_____

3)_____

Today, I am grateful for: Date:

1)_____

2)_____

3)_____

Today, I am grateful for: Date:

1)_____

2)_____

3)_____

This week:

Who made me smile?_____

Who inspired me?_____

What is the best thing that happened?_____

_____

What do I want to attract more of?_____

_____

Week 21

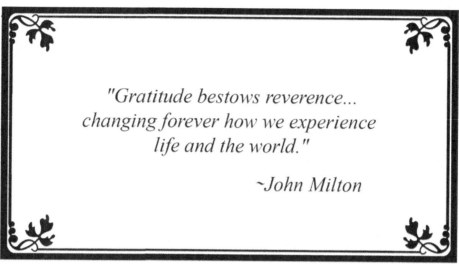

"Gratitude bestows reverence...
changing forever how we experience
life and the world."

~John Milton

Today, I am grateful for: Date:
1)_____
2)_____
3)_____

Today, I am grateful for: Date:
1)_____
2)_____
3)_____

Today, I am grateful for: Date:
1)_____
2)_____
3)_____

Today, I am grateful for: Date:

1)_____

2)_____

3)_____

Today, I am grateful for: Date:

1)_____

2)_____

3)_____

Today, I am grateful for: Date:

1)_____

2)_____

3)_____

Today, I am grateful for: Date:

1)_____

2)_____

3)_____

This week:

Who made me smile?_____

Who inspired me?_____

What is the best thing that happened?_____

_____

What do I want to attract more of?_____

_____

Week 22

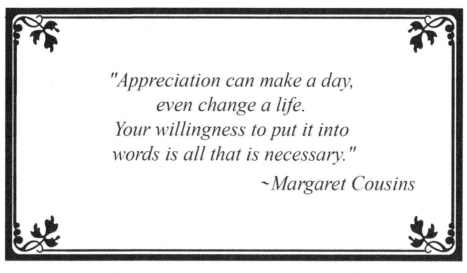

"Appreciation can make a day,
even change a life.
Your willingness to put it into
words is all that is necessary."

~Margaret Cousins

Today, I am grateful for: Date:_____
1)_____
2)_____
3)_____

Today, I am grateful for: Date:_____
1)_____
2)_____
3)_____

Today, I am grateful for: Date:_____
1)_____
2)_____
3)_____

Today, I am grateful for: Date:

1)_____
2)_____
3)_____

Today, I am grateful for: Date:

1)_____
2)_____
3)_____

Today, I am grateful for: Date:

1)_____
2)_____
3)_____

Today, I am grateful for: Date:

1)_____
2)_____
3)_____

This week:

Who made me smile?_____
Who inspired me?_____
What is the best thing that happened?_____
_____
What do I want to attract more of?_____
_____

Week 23

"Forget yesterday - it has already forgotten you.
Don't sweat tomorrow - you haven't even met.
Instead, open your eyes and your
heart to a truly precious gift - today."

~Steve Maraboli

Today, I am grateful for: Date:

1)_____

2)_____

3)_____

Today, I am grateful for: Date:

1)_____

2)_____

3)_____

Today, I am grateful for: Date:

1)_____

2)_____

3)_____

Today, I am grateful for: Date: _____

1)_____

2)_____

3)_____

Today, I am grateful for: Date: _____

1)_____

2)_____

3)_____

Today, I am grateful for: Date: _____

1)_____

2)_____

3)_____

Today, I am grateful for: Date: _____

1)_____

2)_____

3)_____

This week:

Who made me smile?_____

Who inspired me?_____

What is the best thing that happened?_____

_____

What do I want to attract more of?_____

_____

Week 24

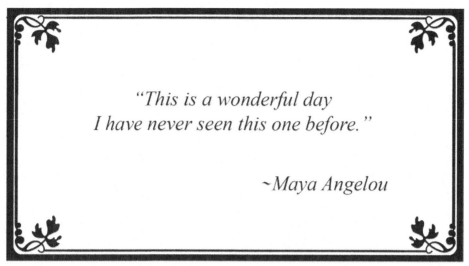

*"This is a wonderful day
I have never seen this one before."*

~Maya Angelou

Today, I am grateful for: Date:
1)_____
2)_____
3)_____

Today, I am grateful for: Date:
1)_____
2)_____
3)_____

Today, I am grateful for: Date:
1)_____
2)_____
3)_____

Today, I am grateful for: _____ Date: _____
1)_____
2)_____
3)_____

Today, I am grateful for: _____ Date: _____
1)_____
2)_____
3)_____

Today, I am grateful for: _____ Date: _____
1)_____
2)_____
3)_____

Today, I am grateful for: _____ Date: _____
1)_____
2)_____
3)_____

This week:

Who made me smile?_____
Who inspired me?_____
What is the best thing that happened?_____
_____
What do I want to attract more of?_____
_____

Week 25

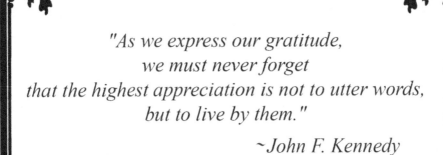

*"As we express our gratitude,
we must never forget
that the highest appreciation is not to utter words,
but to live by them."*

~John F. Kennedy

Today, I am grateful for: Date: _____
1)_____
2)_____
3)_____

Today, I am grateful for: Date: _____
1)_____
2)_____
3)_____

Today, I am grateful for: Date: _____
1)_____
2)_____
3)_____

Today, I am grateful for: Date:_____

1)_____

2)_____

3)_____

Today, I am grateful for: Date:_____

1)_____

2)_____

3)_____

Today, I am grateful for: Date:_____

1)_____

2)_____

3)_____

Today, I am grateful for: Date:_____

1)_____

2)_____

3)_____

This week:

Who made me smile?_____

Who inspired me?_____

What is the best thing that happened?_____
_____

What do I want to attract more of?_____
_____

Week 26

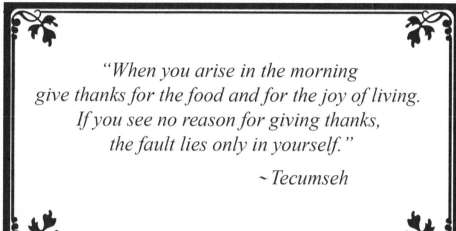

*"When you arise in the morning
give thanks for the food and for the joy of living.
If you see no reason for giving thanks,
the fault lies only in yourself."*

~ Tecumseh

Today, I am grateful for: Date:
1)_____
2)_____
3)_____

Today, I am grateful for: Date:
1)_____
2)_____
3)_____

Today, I am grateful for: Date:
1)_____
2)_____
3)_____

Today, I am grateful for: Date:

1)_____

2)_____

3)_____

Today, I am grateful for: Date:

1)_____

2)_____

3)_____

Today, I am grateful for: Date:

1)_____

2)_____

3)_____

Today, I am grateful for: Date:

1)_____

2)_____

3)_____

This week:

Who made me smile?_____

Who inspired me?_____

What is the best thing that happened?_____

_____

What do I want to attract more of?_____

_____

Week 27

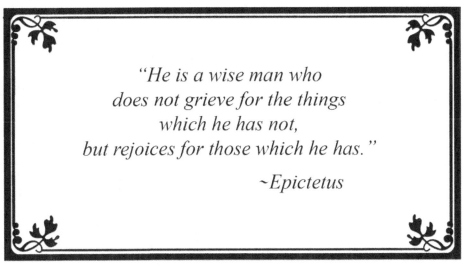

*"He is a wise man who
does not grieve for the things
which he has not,
but rejoices for those which he has."*

~Epictetus

Today, I am grateful for: Date:_____

1)_____
2)_____
3)_____

Today, I am grateful for: Date:_____

1)_____
2)_____
3)_____

Today, I am grateful for: Date:_____

1)_____
2)_____
3)_____

Today, I am grateful for: Date:
1)_____
2)_____
3)_____

Today, I am grateful for: Date:
1)_____
2)_____
3)_____

Today, I am grateful for: Date:
1)_____
2)_____
3)_____

Today, I am grateful for: Date:
1)_____
2)_____
3)_____

This week:

Who made me smile?_____
Who inspired me?_____
What is the best thing that happened?_____
_____
What do I want to attract more of?_____
_____

Week 28

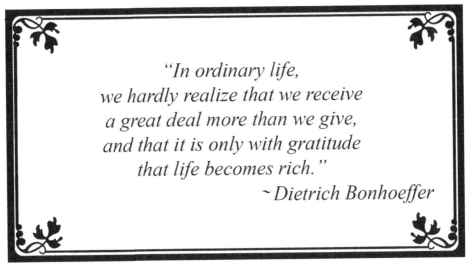

*"In ordinary life,
we hardly realize that we receive
a great deal more than we give,
and that it is only with gratitude
that life becomes rich."*
~*Dietrich Bonhoeffer*

Today, I am grateful for: Date:_____
1)_____
2)_____
3)_____

Today, I am grateful for: Date:_____
1)_____
2)_____
3)_____

Today, I am grateful for: Date:_____
1)_____
2)_____
3)_____

Today, I am grateful for: Date:
1)_____
2)_____
3)_____

Today, I am grateful for: Date:
1)_____
2)_____
3)_____

Today, I am grateful for: Date:
1)_____
2)_____
3)_____

Today, I am grateful for: Date:
1)_____
2)_____
3)_____

This week:

Who made me smile?_____
Who inspired me?_____
What is the best thing that happened?_____
_____
What do I want to attract more of?_____
_____

Week 29

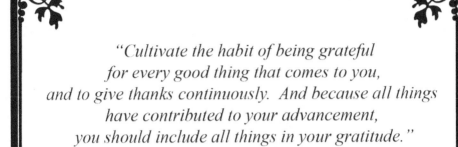

*"Cultivate the habit of being grateful
for every good thing that comes to you,
and to give thanks continuously. And because all things
have contributed to your advancement,
you should include all things in your gratitude."*

~ Ralph Waldo Emerson

Today, I am grateful for: Date:

1)_____

2)_____

3)_____

Today, I am grateful for: Date:

1)_____

2)_____

3)_____

Today, I am grateful for: Date:

1)_____

2)_____

3)_____

Today, I am grateful for: Date:_____

1)_____

2)_____

3)_____

Today, I am grateful for: Date:_____

1)_____

2)_____

3)_____

Today, I am grateful for: Date:_____

1)_____

2)_____

3)_____

Today, I am grateful for: Date:_____

1)_____

2)_____

3)_____

This week:

Who made me smile?_____

Who inspired me?_____

What is the best thing that happened?_____
_____

What do I want to attract more of?_____
_____

Week 30

"If the only prayer you said was thank you,
that would be enough."

~Meister Eckhart

Today, I am grateful for: Date:
1)_____
2)_____
3)_____

Today, I am grateful for: Date:
1)_____
2)_____
3)_____

Today, I am grateful for: Date:
1)_____
2)_____
3)_____

Today, I am grateful for: Date:

1)_____
2)_____
3)_____

Today, I am grateful for: Date:

1)_____
2)_____
3)_____

Today, I am grateful for: Date:

1)_____
2)_____
3)_____

Today, I am grateful for: Date:

1)_____
2)_____
3)_____

This week:

Who made me smile?_____
Who inspired me?_____
What is the best thing that happened?_____
_____
What do I want to attract more of?_____
_____

Week 31

"We must find time to stop and thank the people who make a difference in our lives."

~John F. Kennedy

Today, I am grateful for: Date:
1)_____
2)_____
3)_____

Today, I am grateful for: Date:
1)_____
2)_____
3)_____

Today, I am grateful for: Date:
1)_____
2)_____
3)_____

Today, I am grateful for: Date:

1)_____

2)_____

3)_____

Today, I am grateful for: Date:

1)_____

2)_____

3)_____

Today, I am grateful for: Date:

1)_____

2)_____

3)_____

Today, I am grateful for: Date:

1)_____

2)_____

3)_____

This week:

Who made me smile?_____

Who inspired me?_____

What is the best thing that happened?_____

_____

What do I want to attract more of?_____

_____

Week 32

"*Gratitude is not only the greatest
of virtues, but the parent of all others.*"

~*Marcus Tullius Cicero*

Today, I am grateful for: Date:

1)_____
2)_____
3)_____

Today, I am grateful for: Date:

1)_____
2)_____
3)_____

Today, I am grateful for: Date:

1)_____
2)_____
3)_____

Today, I am grateful for: _____ Date: _____
1)_____
2)_____
3)_____

Today, I am grateful for: _____ Date: _____
1)_____
2)_____
3)_____

Today, I am grateful for: _____ Date: _____
1)_____
2)_____
3)_____

Today, I am grateful for: _____ Date: _____
1)_____
2)_____
3)_____

This week:

Who made me smile?_____
Who inspired me?_____
What is the best thing that happened?_____
_____
What do I want to attract more of?_____
_____

Week 33

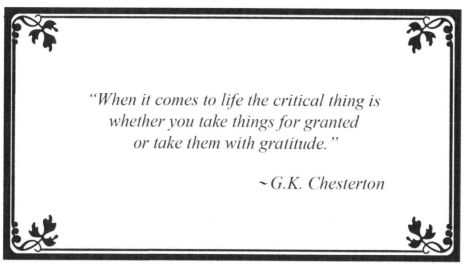

"When it comes to life the critical thing is whether you take things for granted or take them with gratitude."

~ G.K. Chesterton

Today, I am grateful for: Date:

1)_____

2)_____

3)_____

Today, I am grateful for: Date:

1)_____

2)_____

3)_____

Today, I am grateful for: Date:

1)_____

2)_____

3)_____

Today, I am grateful for: _____ Date: _____

1)_____
2)_____
3)_____

Today, I am grateful for: _____ Date: _____

1)_____
2)_____
3)_____

Today, I am grateful for: _____ Date: _____

1)_____
2)_____
3)_____

Today, I am grateful for: _____ Date: _____

1)_____
2)_____
3)_____

This week:

Who made me smile?_____
Who inspired me?_____
What is the best thing that happened?_____
_____
What do I want to attract more of?_____
_____

Week 34

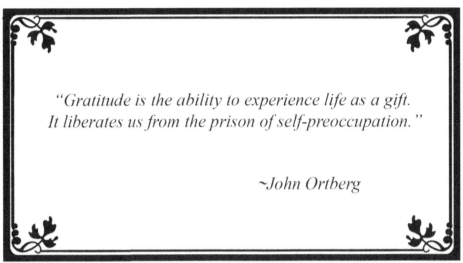

"Gratitude is the ability to experience life as a gift.
It liberates us from the prison of self-preoccupation."

~John Ortberg

Today, I am grateful for: Date:
1)_____
2)_____
3)_____

Today, I am grateful for: Date:
1)_____
2)_____
3)_____

Today, I am grateful for: Date:
1)_____
2)_____
3)_____

Today, I am grateful for: Date:
1)_____
2)_____
3)_____

Today, I am grateful for: Date:
1)_____
2)_____
3)_____

Today, I am grateful for: Date:
1)_____
2)_____
3)_____

Today, I am grateful for: Date:
1)_____
2)_____
3)_____

This week:

Who made me smile?_____
Who inspired me?_____
What is the best thing that happened?_____
_____
What do I want to attract more of?_____
_____

Week 35

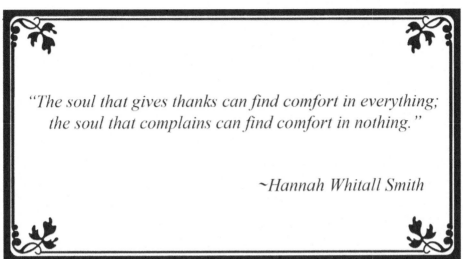

"The soul that gives thanks can find comfort in everything; the soul that complains can find comfort in nothing."

~Hannah Whitall Smith

Today, I am grateful for: Date:_____
1)_____
2)_____
3)_____

Today, I am grateful for: Date:_____
1)_____
2)_____
3)_____

Today, I am grateful for: Date:_____
1)_____
2)_____
3)_____

Today, I am grateful for: Date:

1)_____
2)_____
3)_____

Today, I am grateful for: Date:

1)_____
2)_____
3)_____

Today, I am grateful for: Date:

1)_____
2)_____
3)_____

Today, I am grateful for: Date:

1)_____
2)_____
3)_____

This week:

Who made me smile?_____
Who inspired me?_____
What is the best thing that happened?_____
_____
What do I want to attract more of?_____
_____

Week 36

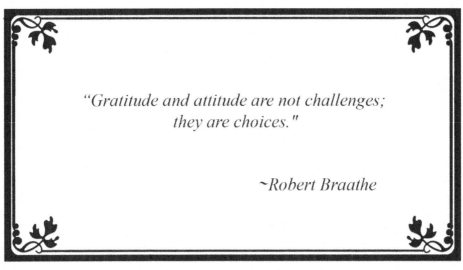

"Gratitude and attitude are not challenges; they are choices."

~Robert Braathe

Today, I am grateful for: Date:
1)
2)
3)

Today, I am grateful for: Date:
1)
2)
3)

Today, I am grateful for: Date:
1)
2)
3)

Today, I am grateful for: _____ Date: _____

1)_____
2)_____
3)_____

Today, I am grateful for: _____ Date: _____

1)_____
2)_____
3)_____

Today, I am grateful for: _____ Date: _____

1)_____
2)_____
3)_____

Today, I am grateful for: _____ Date: _____

1)_____
2)_____
3)_____

This week:

Who made me smile?_____
Who inspired me?_____
What is the best thing that happened?_____
_____
What do I want to attract more of?_____
_____

Week 37

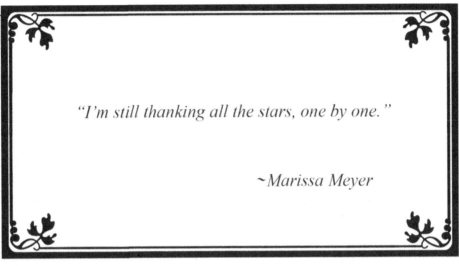

"I'm still thanking all the stars, one by one."

~Marissa Meyer

Today, I am grateful for: Date: _____
1)_____
2)_____
3)_____

Today, I am grateful for: Date: _____
1)_____
2)_____
3)_____

Today, I am grateful for: Date: _____
1)_____
2)_____
3)_____

Today, I am grateful for: Date:
1)_____
2)_____
3)_____

Today, I am grateful for: Date:
1)_____
2)_____
3)_____

Today, I am grateful for: Date:
1)_____
2)_____
3)_____

Today, I am grateful for: Date:
1)_____
2)_____
3)_____

This week:

Who made me smile?_____
Who inspired me?_____
What is the best thing that happened?_____
_____
What do I want to attract more of?_____
_____

Week 38

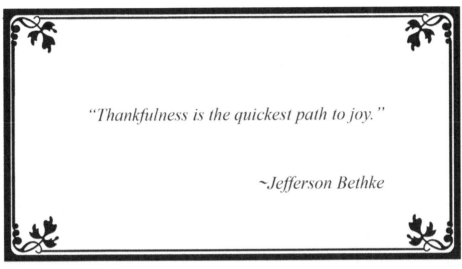

"Thankfulness is the quickest path to joy."

~Jefferson Bethke

Today, I am grateful for: Date: _____
1)_____
2)_____
3)_____

Today, I am grateful for: Date: _____
1)_____
2)_____
3)_____

Today, I am grateful for: Date: _____
1)_____
2)_____
3)_____

Today, I am grateful for: Date:

1)_____

2)_____

3)_____

Today, I am grateful for: Date:

1)_____

2)_____

3)_____

Today, I am grateful for: Date:

1)_____

2)_____

3)_____

Today, I am grateful for: Date:

1)_____

2)_____

3)_____

This week:

Who made me smile?_____

Who inspired me?_____

What is the best thing that happened?_____

_____

What do I want to attract more of?_____

_____

Week 39

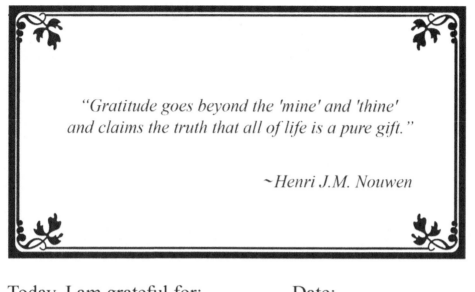

*"Gratitude goes beyond the 'mine' and 'thine'
and claims the truth that all of life is a pure gift."*

~Henri J.M. Nouwen

Today, I am grateful for: Date:

1)_____
2)_____
3)_____

Today, I am grateful for: Date:

1)_____
2)_____
3)_____

Today, I am grateful for: Date:

1)_____
2)_____
3)_____

Today, I am grateful for: Date:

1)_____
2)_____
3)_____

Today, I am grateful for: Date:

1)_____
2)_____
3)_____

Today, I am grateful for: Date:

1)_____
2)_____
3)_____

Today, I am grateful for: Date:

1)_____
2)_____
3)_____

This week:

Who made me smile?_____
Who inspired me?_____
What is the best thing that happened?_____
_____
What do I want to attract more of?_____
_____

Week 40

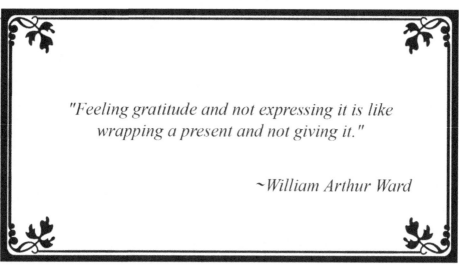

"Feeling gratitude and not expressing it is like wrapping a present and not giving it."

~William Arthur Ward

Today, I am grateful for: Date:
1)_____
2)_____
3)_____

Today, I am grateful for: Date:
1)_____
2)_____
3)_____

Today, I am grateful for: Date:
1)_____
2)_____
3)_____

Today, I am grateful for: Date:

1)_____

2)_____

3)_____

Today, I am grateful for: Date:

1)_____

2)_____

3)_____

Today, I am grateful for: Date:

1)_____

2)_____

3)_____

Today, I am grateful for: Date:

1)_____

2)_____

3)_____

This week:

Who made me smile?_____

Who inspired me?_____

What is the best thing that happened?_____

_____

What do I want to attract more of?_____

_____

Week 41

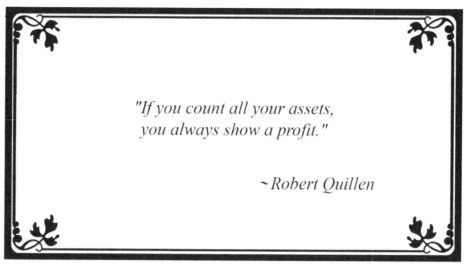

"If you count all your assets,
you always show a profit."

~Robert Quillen

Today, I am grateful for: Date:
1)_____
2)_____
3)_____

Today, I am grateful for: Date:
1)_____
2)_____
3)_____

Today, I am grateful for: Date:
1)_____
2)_____
3)_____

Today, I am grateful for: Date: _____

1)_____
2)_____
3)_____

Today, I am grateful for: Date: _____

1)_____
2)_____
3)_____

Today, I am grateful for: Date: _____

1)_____
2)_____
3)_____

Today, I am grateful for: Date: _____

1)_____
2)_____
3)_____

This week:

Who made me smile?_____
Who inspired me?_____
What is the best thing that happened?_____
_____
What do I want to attract more of?_____
_____

Week 42

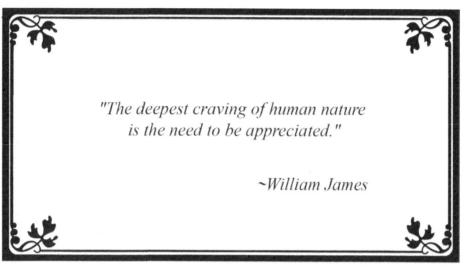

*"The deepest craving of human nature
is the need to be appreciated."*

~William James

Today, I am grateful for: Date:
1)_____
2)_____
3)_____

Today, I am grateful for: Date:
1)_____
2)_____
3)_____

Today, I am grateful for: Date:
1)_____
2)_____
3)_____

Today, I am grateful for: Date:
1)_____
2)_____
3)_____

Today, I am grateful for: Date:
1)_____
2)_____
3)_____

Today, I am grateful for: Date:
1)_____
2)_____
3)_____

Today, I am grateful for: Date:
1)_____
2)_____
3)_____

This week:

Who made me smile?_____
Who inspired me?_____
What is the best thing that happened?_____
_____
What do I want to attract more of?_____
_____

Week 43

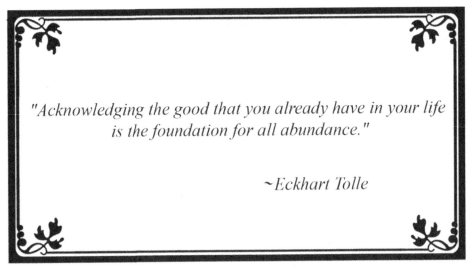

"Acknowledging the good that you already have in your life is the foundation for all abundance."

~Eckhart Tolle

Today, I am grateful for: Date: _____

1)_____

2)_____

3)_____

Today, I am grateful for: Date: _____

1)_____

2)_____

3)_____

Today, I am grateful for: Date: _____

1)_____

2)_____

3)_____

Today, I am grateful for: Date:

1)_____

2)_____

3)_____

Today, I am grateful for: Date:

1)_____

2)_____

3)_____

Today, I am grateful for: Date:

1)_____

2)_____

3)_____

Today, I am grateful for: Date:

1)_____

2)_____

3)_____

This week:

Who made me smile?_____

Who inspired me?_____

What is the best thing that happened?_____

_____

What do I want to attract more of?_____

_____

Week 44

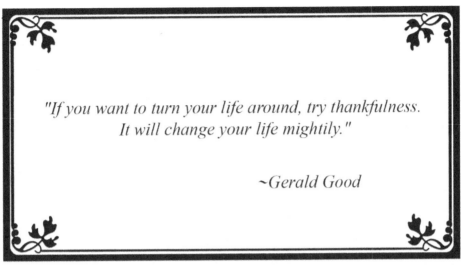

*"If you want to turn your life around, try thankfulness.
It will change your life mightily."*

~Gerald Good

Today, I am grateful for: Date:_____

1)_____

2)_____

3)_____

Today, I am grateful for: Date:_____

1)_____

2)_____

3)_____

Today, I am grateful for: Date:_____

1)_____

2)_____

3)_____

Today, I am grateful for: Date:

1)_____

2)_____

3)_____

Today, I am grateful for: Date:

1)_____

2)_____

3)_____

Today, I am grateful for: Date:

1)_____

2)_____

3)_____

Today, I am grateful for: Date:

1)_____

2)_____

3)_____

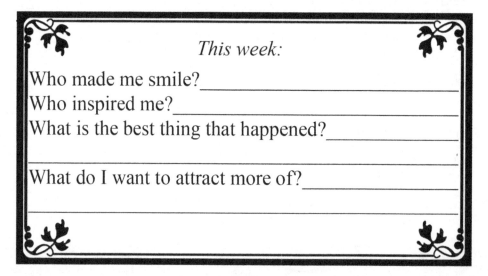

This week:

Who made me smile?_____

Who inspired me?_____

What is the best thing that happened?_____
_____

What do I want to attract more of?_____
_____

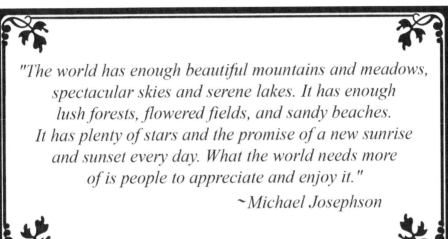

"The world has enough beautiful mountains and meadows, spectacular skies and serene lakes. It has enough lush forests, flowered fields, and sandy beaches. It has plenty of stars and the promise of a new sunrise and sunset every day. What the world needs more of is people to appreciate and enjoy it."

~Michael Josephson

Today, I am grateful for: Date:

1)_____

2)_____

3)_____

Today, I am grateful for: Date:

1)_____

2)_____

3)_____

Today, I am grateful for: Date:

1)_____

2)_____

3)_____

Today, I am grateful for: Date:
1)_____
2)_____
3)_____

Today, I am grateful for: Date:
1)_____
2)_____
3)_____

Today, I am grateful for: Date:
1)_____
2)_____
3)_____

Today, I am grateful for: Date:
1)_____
2)_____
3)_____

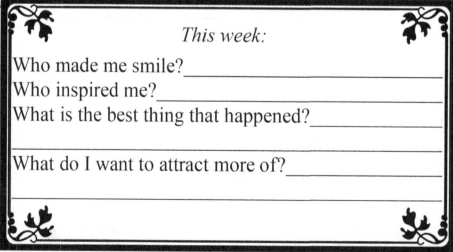

This week:

Who made me smile?_____
Who inspired me?_____
What is the best thing that happened?_____
_____
What do I want to attract more of?_____
_____

Week 46

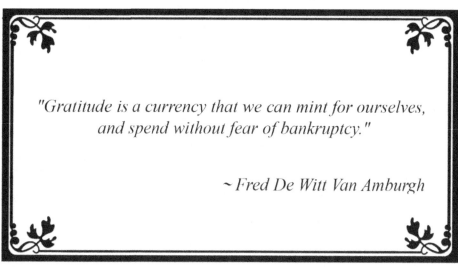

"Gratitude is a currency that we can mint for ourselves, and spend without fear of bankruptcy."

~ Fred De Witt Van Amburgh

Today, I am grateful for: Date:
1)_____
2)_____
3)_____

Today, I am grateful for: Date:
1)_____
2)_____
3)_____

Today, I am grateful for: Date:
1)_____
2)_____
3)_____

Today, I am grateful for: Date:_____

1)_____

2)_____

3)_____

Today, I am grateful for: Date:_____

1)_____

2)_____

3)_____

Today, I am grateful for: Date:_____

1)_____

2)_____

3)_____

Today, I am grateful for: Date:_____

1)_____

2)_____

3)_____

This week:

Who made me smile?_____

Who inspired me?_____

What is the best thing that happened?_____

_____

What do I want to attract more of?_____

_____

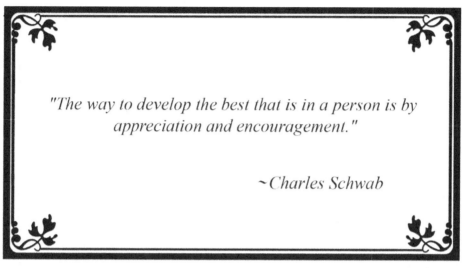

"The way to develop the best that is in a person is by appreciation and encouragement."

~Charles Schwab

Today, I am grateful for: Date: _____
1)_____
2)_____
3)_____

Today, I am grateful for: Date: _____
1)_____
2)_____
3)_____

Today, I am grateful for: Date: _____
1)_____
2)_____
3)_____

Today, I am grateful for: _____ Date: _____

1)_____
2)_____
3)_____

Today, I am grateful for: _____ Date: _____

1)_____
2)_____
3)_____

Today, I am grateful for: _____ Date: _____

1)_____
2)_____
3)_____

Today, I am grateful for: _____ Date: _____

1)_____
2)_____
3)_____

This week:

Who made me smile?_____
Who inspired me?_____
What is the best thing that happened?_____
_____
What do I want to attract more of?_____
_____

Week 48

*"At times, our own light goes out
and is rekindled by a spark from another person.
Each of us has cause to think with deep gratitude of those
who have lighted the flame within us."*

~Albert Schweitzer

Today, I am grateful for: Date:_____
1)_____
2)_____
3)_____

Today, I am grateful for: Date:_____
1)_____
2)_____
3)_____

Today, I am grateful for: Date:_____
1)_____
2)_____
3)_____

Today, I am grateful for: Date:
1)_____
2)_____
3)_____

Today, I am grateful for: Date:
1)_____
2)_____
3)_____

Today, I am grateful for: Date:
1)_____
2)_____
3)_____

Today, I am grateful for: Date:
1)_____
2)_____
3)_____

This week:

Who made me smile?_____
Who inspired me?_____
What is the best thing that happened?_____
_____
What do I want to attract more of?_____
_____

Week 49

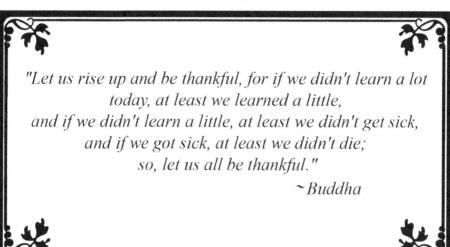

"Let us rise up and be thankful, for if we didn't learn a lot today, at least we learned a little, and if we didn't learn a little, at least we didn't get sick, and if we got sick, at least we didn't die; so, let us all be thankful."

~Buddha

Today, I am grateful for: Date:
1)_____
2)_____
3)_____

Today, I am grateful for: Date:
1)_____
2)_____
3)_____

Today, I am grateful for: Date:
1)_____
2)_____
3)_____

Today, I am grateful for: Date: _____

1)_____

2)_____

3)_____

Today, I am grateful for: Date: _____

1)_____

2)_____

3)_____

Today, I am grateful for: Date: _____

1)_____

2)_____

3)_____

Today, I am grateful for: Date: _____

1)_____

2)_____

3)_____

This week:

Who made me smile?_____

Who inspired me?_____

What is the best thing that happened?_____

_____

What do I want to attract more of?_____

_____

Week 50

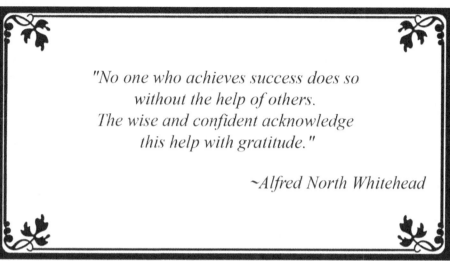

"No one who achieves success does so without the help of others. The wise and confident acknowledge this help with gratitude."

~Alfred North Whitehead

Today, I am grateful for: Date:_____
1)_____
2)_____
3)_____

Today, I am grateful for: Date:_____
1)_____
2)_____
3)_____

Today, I am grateful for: Date:_____
1)_____
2)_____
3)_____

Today, I am grateful for: Date:_____

1)_____

2)_____

3)_____

Today, I am grateful for: Date:_____

1)_____

2)_____

3)_____

Today, I am grateful for: Date:_____

1)_____

2)_____

3)_____

Today, I am grateful for: Date:_____

1)_____

2)_____

3)_____

This week:

Who made me smile?_____

Who inspired me?_____

What is the best thing that happened?_____

_____

What do I want to attract more of?_____

_____

Week 51

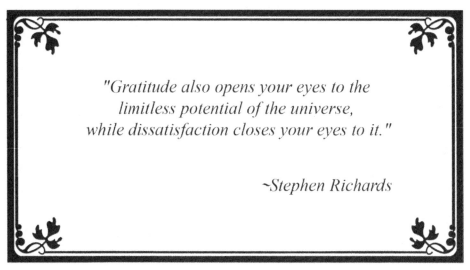

*"Gratitude also opens your eyes to the
limitless potential of the universe,
while dissatisfaction closes your eyes to it."*

~Stephen Richards

Today, I am grateful for: Date:
1)_____
2)_____
3)_____

Today, I am grateful for: Date:
1)_____
2)_____
3)_____

Today, I am grateful for: Date:
1)_____
2)_____
3)_____

Today, I am grateful for: Date:_____
1)_____
2)_____
3)_____

Today, I am grateful for: Date:_____
1)_____
2)_____
3)_____

Today, I am grateful for: Date:_____
1)_____
2)_____
3)_____

Today, I am grateful for: Date:_____
1)_____
2)_____
3)_____

This week:

Who made me smile?_____
Who inspired me?_____
What is the best thing that happened?_____
_____
What do I want to attract more of?_____
_____

Week 52

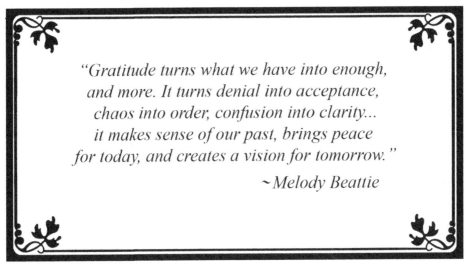

"Gratitude turns what we have into enough, and more. It turns denial into acceptance, chaos into order, confusion into clarity... it makes sense of our past, brings peace for today, and creates a vision for tomorrow."

~Melody Beattie

Today, I am grateful for: Date: _____
1)_____
2)_____
3)_____

Today, I am grateful for: Date: _____
1)_____
2)_____
3)_____

Today, I am grateful for: Date: _____
1)_____
2)_____
3)_____

Today, I am grateful for: _____ Date: _____
1)_____
2)_____
3)_____

Today, I am grateful for: _____ Date: _____
1)_____
2)_____
3)_____

Today, I am grateful for: _____ Date: _____
1)_____
2)_____
3)_____

Today, I am grateful for: _____ Date: _____
1)_____
2)_____
3)_____

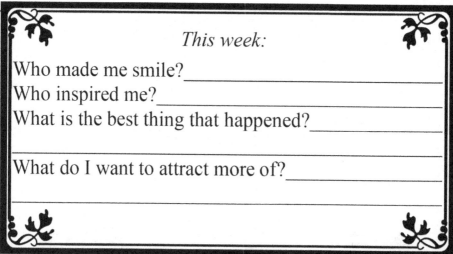

This week:

Who made me smile?_____
Who inspired me?_____
What is the best thing that happened?_____
_____
What do I want to attract more of?_____
_____

Congratulations on finishing
One Year of Gratitude Journaling!

I hope your life has been enriched and that
you continue to practice gratitude daily so that
you can live your best possible life!

Bookmarks

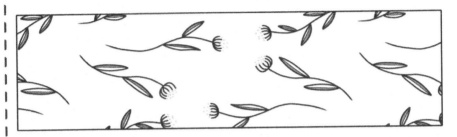

Made in the USA
Las Vegas, NV
14 November 2024

11805509R00184